CONTACTS

Maggie passed over the magazine; the word *Contacts* was printed across the cover. Amanda flicked it open. Inside, the small ads were set in columns, each accompanied by a photograph. There were pictures of singles and couples, the men in posing pouches, the women in everything from basques to G-strings. Some were completely nude.

'What's this?' said Amanda.

'A way of contacting like-minded people. Ones who are interested in sex.'

'I didn't think you had trouble finding men.'

'Sometimes this is easier – and more exciting. I see a man I fancy and that's it. No emotional claptrap. He knows all I want is sex. I know that's all he wants too. It's ideal for you, Mandy. You can get laid with no complications . . .'

Also available from Headline Delta

Contacts

Becky Bell

Delta

Copyright © 1998 Becky Bell

The right of Becky Bell to be identified as the Author
of the Work has been asserted by her in accordance with the
Copyright, Designs and Patents Act 1988.

First published in 1998
by HEADLINE BOOK PUBLISHING

A HEADLINE DELTA paperback

10 9 8 7 6 5 4 3 2 1

ISBN 0 7472 5650 0

Typeset by Palimpsest Book Production Limited,
Polmont, Stirlingshire
Printed and bound in Great Britain by
Mackays of Chatham PLC, Chatham, Kent

HEADLINE BOOK PUBLISHING
A division of Hodder Headline PLC
338 Euston Road
London NW1 3BH

Contacts

Chapter One

'So, what did you do then?'

'I was very bold. I told him I thought he was gorgeous and asked him to take me to bed.'

'Just like that?'

'Of course. There's no point beating about the bush is there?'

'And?'

'I told you, I'd got all dressed up like a dog's dinner. I mean, I had this slinky black dress with a skirt split up to the thigh and one of those bras that make your cleavage look like the Panama Canal. So, as I got into the car the skirt fell open and he got a good look at my thighs. And my black stockings, the shiny ones with the lacy tops. His eyes nearly popped out of his head.'

'I bet.'

'Naturally, I didn't bother to fold the skirt back. Actually I managed to work it up a bit so he could just see my panties.'

'I'm surprised you were wearing any,' Amanda Landseer said, laughing. Maggie O'Keefe never failed to amaze her.

'I'd thought about it, but I decided on a more subtle approach.'

Maggie was a tall, statuesque woman with a figure most women would die for, and a strong, slightly masculine face with a straight nose and high cheekbones. Her large sparkling brown eyes reflected her no-nonsense attitude to life. At the moment the ample curves of her body and her long legs were encased in bright yellow Lycra that clung to every contour, emphasising in particular her big breasts. Her thick, jet-black hair was cut to an equal length just above her shoulders, its healthy sheen catching the light.

'And?' Amanda asked impatiently.

'Naturally, he had a great deal of trouble keeping his eyes on the road. He asked me if I always wore stockings. I asked him if he liked them and he sort of moaned. So I put my hand down between his legs.'

'Christ, Maggie, you'd only known him an hour.'

'So? I was very attracted to him.' Maggie was a public-relations consultant for an advertising agency and had met the man at a party for one of their client companies who made swimwear. He was a designer.

'What did he do?'

'There wasn't much he could do. He was driving. He had a hard-on, I'm delighted to say. So I asked him if he was uncomfortable then unzipped his fly and got it out.'

'You didn't?'

'Well, I was creaming too. It was a nice one. Big and very thick. I asked him if he'd mind if I sucked it. He nearly crashed the car.'

'I bet.'

'So he pulled over. Fortunately it was a dark street. The controls for the electric seats were in between the armrests so I pressed the button and his seat started to recline. Perfect. There he was in all his glory. I slipped it into my mouth and gave him a really good suck. He was squirming and groaning like he was in pain. But he was hard. Like steel. Lovely. Unfortunately there were too many people about. I mean, we'd left the party early and there were a lot of people walking about and peering into the car.'

'I didn't think that would have stopped you.'

'You're right, I found it quite exciting. I've always liked being watched. If only I'd known.'

'Known what?'

'I'll get to that later. Anyway it wasn't very comfortable. So I let him up and promised I'd behave until he got me home.'

With anyone else, Amanda might have suspected that Maggie was spicing the story up but they'd been friends since she moved in next door two years ago and she knew the woman was not one for exaggeration.

'So he drove home, like a bat out of hell,' Maggie continued. 'with his cock hanging out of his trousers.'

'And your legs still on display?'

'Naturally. Do you want another glass of wine?' They were curled up in big comfortable armchairs in the front room of Maggie's large Victorian terraced house, a bottle of Cabernet Sauvignon opened on the coffee table in front of them. It was a warm spring evening and the French windows were open on to the garden, a pleasant scent of flowers drifting in on a light breeze.

'Thanks.'

Maggie lent forward and refreshed their glasses.

'Anyway, he's got this beautiful penthouse apartment in Highgate. Fantastic views. Luckily there's a garage in the basement and we went up in the lift.'

'What, with his thingy still . . . ?'

'Sticking out of his trousers, yes. I don't know why but that really turned me on. The moment we got inside his flat I just couldn't contain myself. I practically threw him to the floor. Didn't even bother to take my knickers off. Just hopped on top of him and pulled them aside. I was slicker than a jar of cold cream and I bounced up and down on him, like I was demented. He was so big. Filled me right up. Right here.' She dug her fingers into her belly. 'And you know me. Come at the drop of a sailor's trousers. I think I came three times just in the hall.'

'But he didn't?' Amanda asked.

'No. It's great. He didn't. He was still as hard as a rock. When I'd calmed down a bit, he helped me up and lead me into the front room. Asked me if I wanted a drink. Believe me, I needed a brandy.'

'And?'

'He started to strip his clothes off. Very unselfconscious. He's got a great body. Big broad chest covered in a mat of hair. Thick muscles like cords of rope. Lovely. When he was nude he poured two drinks and brought them over, his cock sticking out like a poker. Then he sat down and looked up at me, like it was my turn to strip. So I did. I had a big gulp of brandy, and it was really good stuff, then put the glass down and started unzipping my dress. I put one foot up on the coffee table right in front of him so my skirt fell open and he could see my stockings again, then I peeled my dress away. I saw his eyes moving from my thighs to my bra, like he couldn't decide where to look next. When I slipped out of my bra – and you know I'm very well endowed in that department – I just stood there in my little black suspender belt and these thong cut panties and let him get a real eyeful.'

'I don't think I could ever do anything like that.'

'Of course you could. It's a turn-on.'

'And he just sat there?'

'Yes. He sipped his brandy and just looked at me. Funnily enough, I found that very sexy.'

'You find everything sexy.'

'True. Anyway, I slipped my panties off and knelt on the sofa, right on top of him. By that time I was really in the mood again. And he obviously was. I held his cheeks in my hands and kissed him on the mouth while I pressed myself down on that lovely big erection. God, it felt good. But that's when it happened.'

'What?'

'I was, like, gone – I mean coming again. His tongue was in my mouth and his cock in my pussy. Wonderful. I had my eyes closed and I was quivering. I must have heard a noise. I opened my eyes and there was another guy standing in the doorway behind the sofa. He'd got this expression on his face that's like mild interest, as if we were some diverting exhibit in a museum. I don't know why but if he'd been drooling at the mouth it would have been a turn-off, but the way he was so cool about it just put me into orbit. My whole body seemed to clench and I had this incredible orgasm.'

'Who was he?'

'A friend staying for the weekend. An old schoolfriend.'

'Did he apologise?'

'No. When I came round, Robert, that's the guy I'm sitting on, calmly introduced us, like it was perfectly normal for us to be copulating while I said hello to his friend. We actually shook hands! And then he sat down in a chair opposite, obviously not intending to leave.'

'So, what then – you stormed out?'

'I suppose I should have done. But to tell you the truth the thought of walking out never crossed my mind. I had Robert's cock buried inside me and the fact that this guy was watching was an extra thrill. It was for Robert too. I swear he'd got harder and bigger. So I start riding him again. I thought I was turned on before but this was completely different. I was coming continuously. And I could feel Robert's cock beginning to spasm. That and those cool eyes boring into me . . . well, I don't think it's ever been better.'

'You always say that.'

'It's always true. Sex gets better and better as far as I'm concerned.'

'I wish I could say the same. So did this other guy join in?'

'What a suggestion!' Maggie mimed shock.

'Come on let's have the whole sordid story.'

'I felt as if I couldn't take anymore. I sort of collapsed on the sofa, curled up into a ball of pleasure. I don't know how long it was before I could be bothered to do anything but wallow in the aftermath of what he'd done to me. Eventually I rolled over and this guy, Tom he was called, was standing looking down at me. He was naked and he'd got his cock in his hand, wanking it up and down with his eyes a glued to my thighs. He was young, I mean only about twenty, and perhaps he'd never seen black stockings before. So I turned around and lay on my back and slowly opened my legs, you know, like an invitation. I could see his cock pulsing.'

'And what was happening to Robert?'

'He was still sitting at the end of the sofa, with his brandy glass in his hand. Tom looked a bit scared, like he was afraid to do anything. So I told Tom that it was perfectly all right. That I'd like it if he put his lovely big cock right up me. And he did. Naturally I was wetter than I've ever been but it didn't put him off. He started hammering into me. Over his shoulder I could see Robert watching us. I wrapped my legs around Tom's back. One of my suspenders popped. I knew it wasn't going to take him long. But it wasn't going to take me long either. The feeling of him against all that sticky wetness was incredible. But it was the thought of it that was the biggest turn-on. The idea of having these two men one after the other, and them both spunking me. Christ, just talking about it is making me wet again.'

'Maggie!'

'Well, it's true. I'm going to have to go and change.'

'And is that it?'

'Not really. But let's skip over the rest.'

'Let's not. I want to hear it all.'

'Put it this way. The recovery rate of the young is remarkable. By the time Tom's finished with me, or I've finished with him, Robert's was hard as he was in the first place. So I suggested that maybe they'd like to take me somewhere more comfortable. We ended up on this king-sized bed with me in the middle. After Robert had another go, Tom got it up again. Wonderful. What more could any woman want?'

'You're incorrigible.'

'Life's not a rehearsal. And they took me to breakfast at the Savoy next morning.'

'When was this?'

'Last Saturday. I could hardly walk all weekend.'

'I vaguely remember that feeling.'

'Only vaguely?'

'Greg's not very enthusiastic anymore. Five years of marriage seems to have dulled his appetites. He used to be really good at it. But now he just doesn't seem to find me attractive anymore. Sounds like a letter to an agony aunt doesn't it?'

'Have you tried to spice things up?'

'God, yes. I spent a fortune on lingerie. Dressed up like a first-class whore. I even met him at the front door in a pair of red high heels and hold-ups and nothing else. Oh, he took me to bed, but it didn't last long. Ten minutes and he's downstairs watching his favourite soap. The trouble is, I really like sex. I always have. I used to be quite good at it too. Now I can't remember the last time I had a really good orgasm, you know, the sort when the earth moves.'

'Pity. Greg's an attractive man.'

'That only makes it worse.'

Maggie leant forward and poured the remains of the wine into their glasses. She got up and went through into the kitchen to get another bottle.

'Well there're these counsellors now, for married couples.'

She put the bottle back into the room and opened it, then topped up the glasses.

'He'd never agree to that.'

'In that case you've got two choices.'

'Which are?' Amanda picked up her glass and drank the wine. It had begun to taste a little sour.

'Divorce or a fling.'

'Basically, I like Greg. He's a nice man.'

'Then have a fling.'

'What if he found out?'

'Be careful.'

'I'm not very good at lying.'

'Get good at it. You can do anything if you try. It doesn't have to be a serious affair, just sex.' Maggie got up again and went to a small bookcase that was crammed with books. She extracted a small, thin magazine from between the tomes. 'Here, look at this.'

She handed it to Amanda. The cover was nondescript, plastered with cut-outs of small ads, its title, in large white lettering printed diagonally across the page: CONTACTS. Amanda flicked it open. Inside, the small ads were set in columns, each accompanied by a black-and-white photograph. She stared at them in amazement. They were pictures of singles and couples. Some were scantily clad in underwear, the men in posing pouches, the women in everything from basques with stockings and suspenders, to G-strings and lacy bodies and bras. Others were completely nude. More than that, most of the women were lying or bending over with their legs wide open so their vaginas were completely exposed. Some even held their labia open for the camera so the mouth of their sex was visible. Some had their breasts in their hands, squeezing them together or pushing them up towards their mouth intent on showing they were big enough for them to be able to suck their own nipples. The men were less obvious. Most were not erect and stood looking uncomfortable. One or two had large hard-ons and stood side on to the camera presumably in an effort to emphasise the length of their phalluses.

'What's this?' Amanda asked, flicking through the pages.

'What it says. It's a way of contacting like-minded people. Ones who are interested in sex.'

'Have you used this?'

'That would be telling.'

'Don't be coy.'

'Of course I've used it. Why do you think I've got it in the house?'

'I didn't think you had any trouble finding men.'

'I don't. But sometimes . . . well, sometimes this is easier. And more exciting. I see a man I fancy and that's it. No emotional claptrap. No wondering what's going to happen at the end of the evening. He knows all I want is sex. I know that's all he wants too.'

'Just like that.'

'Just like that. It's ideal for you, Mandy. You can get laid with no complications. You don't even have to use your own name. And you can use my telephone number if you want. He doesn't even have to know where you live, so there's no risk.'

'It's still cheating. I've never cheated on Greg. And I'm pretty sure he's never cheated on me.'

'Come on, Mandy. Sex isn't something you can just forget about. If you're not getting it at home sooner or later you start looking around for it elsewhere. And if you want my advice it's better to do it this way, with no involvement, than get so desperate that in a couple of years' time you confuse lust with love. You could find yourself in bed with someone you start imagining you're in love with just because he's given you a good time.'

Amanda thought about that. It made sense. She flicked through the pages of the booklet again. This time she noticed how many of the photographs were couples, though they were not often photographed together, two different pictures cropped to fit side by side, each, presumably, taken by the other partner.

'I can't,' she said decisively, closing the booklet and putting it down on the coffee table.

'Fine. But do me a favour would you?'

'What?'

'Just take it with you. Think about it. Read some of the ads. If you still don't want to do anything about it there's no problem. But at least think about it. I tell you, Mandy, if you feel sexually frustrated now, it's only going to get worse. And the more desperate you get the more likely it is you'll do something silly.'

'Like what?'

'Like getting involved with someone totally wrong for you just because he's got a big dick.'

Amanda laughed. 'Sounds good to me.'

'If all you want is sex then that's the answer.' Maggie picked up *Contacts* and handed it back to her friend.

'So, what you're saying, basically, is this little book can save my marriage.'

'Exactly. If you're frustrated. And you know you are or you wouldn't have brought the matter up.'

Amanda looked at her watch. 'I'd better be going. I've got to think about dinner.' She got to her feet, feeling the effect of the wine they had drunk. 'I think I've had too much to drink.'

'It helped loosen your tongue.'

'Just between you and me, right?'

'Of course.' Maggie got to her feet, unfurling her long legs. The Lycra body was so tight it had folded itself into the lips of her sex.

'When do you want this back?' Amanda held up *Contacts*.

'Keep it. There's a new edition every month. I subscribe.' Her face broke into a mischievous grin. 'But don't let Greg find it.'

'I won't.'

They kissed at the front door and Amanda walked down the front path, out of the little wicket gate and up her own path to her front door.

'Bye,' she called as she opened the door.

The phone rang five minutes later. Amanda answered it in the kitchen.

'Sweetheart, I'm going to be late.' It was her husband.

'How late?' Amanda was not annoyed. In fact she was delighted. It gave her a chance to sober up.

'Couple of hours. I should be home by ten.'

'Fine.'

'We could go to the Italian, if you like.'

'Let's just have a salad and some cheese.'

'Perfect. See you later. You are all right? You sound a bit odd.'

'I'm fine. Just been in to see Maggie.'

'That explains it.'

'Does it?'

'—*Vino veritas*. How many bottles this time?'

'One,' she lied.

'I bet. See you later.'

They exchanged goodbyes and Amanda put the phone down. She sat at the kitchen table, glad of the excuse not to have to do any cooking. She'd left *Contacts* on the table and the cover stared up at her. She picked it up and opened it at random.

Young male, 23, good physique, well-endowed, seeks fulfilling sexual partnerships with women of any age and type. Loves lingerie, and high heels. Good at oral. 45 67 66.

The photograph above the ad was of a slim, naked male with his hands held behind his back. His flaccid penis was not circumcised and his foreskin covered his glans. He had a thick thatch of curly black, pubic hair. Like most of the photographs in the magazine though by no means all, the picture was cropped at the neck so the head was not visible.

As Amanda looked at the naked man she felt her clitoris flex. Maggie's graphic description of her Saturday night encounter had given Amanda a sort of sickly feeling in the pit of her stomach that she was sure had translated itself into a wetness in her sex.

She turned the page.

Attractive couple, early thirties, seek friendly couple for swapping and mutual activities. Cleanliness and discretion assured. Can accommodate. Home counties area. 33 21 45.

The picture above this ad was of a woman in a dark basque,

its suspenders clipped onto grey stockings. She wore black stiletto heels and was half turned away from the camera so her face was hidden but her buttocks were not. They were fleshy and pert and, as she was not wearing panties, Amanda could see wisps of pubic hair between them. She had her hand on her hips and her wedding ring was prominent. There was no photograph of her husband.

Amanda looked further down the page.

Attractive, happily married couple into all sex games looking for like minded couples or singles of either sex. Party invitations welcome. 54 90 10.

This was accompanied by two photographs, pasted together. There was a rather stout but muscular nude man, with a hairless, very smooth body, his hand covering his penis. Next to this was a photograph of a woman. She was sitting on the edge of a bed wearing a transparent white lacy negligee which fastened at the front with a single bow. Her small breasts and dark nipples were clearly visible through it. She wore lurex stockings and her legs were splayed apart to reveal her sex, her pubic hair completely covering her labia and her mons.

Sexy blonde, 21, looking for well-endowed men for evenings of fun. Photographic sessions possible. Loves o. Husband approves and would like to watch. 34 11 56.

Sensuous black man, 28, wishes to meet attractive women. I am proud of my body. Let me share it with you. Your place only. 22 65 98.

Amanda realised that each ad was provoking a reaction in her sex. She could feel a sticky wetness seeping into her panties, and her nipples were as hard as stone. She found herself examining each photograph carefully, imagining what it would be like to see the semi-naked or naked bodies in real life. How would it feel to be so blatant about sex? After all if she phoned the voice-mail system and arranged to meet one of the advertisers there could be no doubt what the agenda was going to be.

She had been with several men before she married Greg but, though it had often been obvious that the evening would end in sex, it had never been as calculated and straightforward as it would be if she decided to call one of these numbers. Oddly, perhaps, the directness of it was exciting. She found herself wondering what she would say and how she would feel. She even started thinking about what she would wear.

It was eight o'clock. Amanda decided she'd have a shower. She went up to the bedroom and the en suite bathroom at the back of it and stripped off her clothes. Naked she gazed at herself in the mirror, imagining how she would look in one of the small black and white photographs. She posed this way and that, mimicking the positions the advertisers had used. She had small but shapely breasts with very dark nipples and virtually no aureolae. Her pubic hair was short and sparse and her belly flat. Undoubtedly her legs were her best feature. They were long and contoured, the thighs moulded by the exercises she did religiously every morning. She stood on tip-toe and half turned, like the woman in the first photograph she had seen. The effort emphasised the crease under her buttocks and shaped her calf muscles.

She stared at her face. She had short, flaxen blonde hair cut into layers, large blue eyes. Her mouth was small and she had very smooth lips. Her nose was slightly *retroussé* and she had sharp, high cheekbones and a small chin. It was a face that had won her many admirers.

She showered quickly hoping to wash away her desire. She did not succeed. As she came back into the bedroom with a towel wrapped around her body she saw *Contacts* lying where she had dropped it on the counterpane. Like a magnet exerting an invisible attraction, it seemed to demand her attention.

She lay on the bed and picked it up, turning on the bedside lamp.

Attractive couple, m29/f22, seek females/couples/good looking men for sexy time. Both love oral and sexy undies. Travel or accommodate. London area. Wife very definitely AC/DC 75 08 32.

Amanda felt her heart lurch as she read the last words. AC/DC. It had not occurred to her that the single females some of the couples were looking for were intended to satisfy the lesbian leanings of the wife, presumably while the husband looked on. She stared at the picture that accompanied the ad. Though the man appeared to be standing next to his wife it was obvious the two pictures had been pasted together and had been taken separately.

The man was wearing a pair of black briefs, his hand posed rather awkwardly on his stomach. His body was not particularly muscular but he was not fat and his chest was covered in thin blond hair. His wife was wearing a plunge-fronted white bra pushing her big breasts together. Below it a white suspender belt cut across her waist, its suspenders extending down from triangular shaped wedges of lace. Bisecting the thin satin suspenders was the even thinner satin ribbon that held a lace panel over her bush. The welts of her black stockings were clipped into the suspenders, but only the tops of her thighs were visible, the photograph having been cropped well above the knee. Neither of the couples's faces were exposed either but Amanda could see the woman's rather sharp chin and the bob of black hair behind her neck.

She stared at the woman's body. Her breasts ballooned out of the bra. The lacy panel that covered her mons revealed a hint of dark pubic hair. The woman held her arms behind her back. It was not difficult to imagine her reaching up to unclip the bra.

Amanda felt a pulse deep in her sex.

Since Maggie had moved in next door, they had told each other everything about their lives without embarrassment, confident in the knowledge that it would go no further. As far as Amanda was concerned they had developed a firm and enduring friendship and one she valued highly. But there was something she had never told anyone about herself, not even Maggie.

Her first job after leaving school had been at a travel agency, a one-woman business. One evening she had been waiting in the office with her boss for confirmation of a large block-booking in a Los Angeles hotel. It was nine o'clock by the time the confirmation came through. Her boss had asked if she would like to come out and eat and they'd gone to the local French restaurant. Monica Morris was an elegant, chestnut-haired woman in her late thirties. Amanda was eighteen. Over dinner they had talked easily and Monica invited her back to her flat for coffee. Amanda accepted the invitation with alacrity. Over coffee Monica asked her if she was a virgin. Amanda told her she was not. Then Monica asked her if she had ever been to bed with another woman. Again, Amanda told her she had not.

She could remember exactly what happened next. If she was truthful with herself – which she wasn't always when it came to sex – she had to admit she played through the whole experience in her mind quite often. Sometimes, though not always, she had allowed herself to dwell on the details when Greg and other men had been making love to her. Though she was loath to admit it, the memory never failed to excite her.

Monica had leant over and touched her cheek.

'You wouldn't be frightened though, would you?' she had said confidently. 'You wouldn't be frightened if I took you to my bed.'

And she wasn't.

Monica had stood up and pulled her to her feet too. Very delicately she'd kissed her on the lips at exactly the same time as her hand moved over Amanda's right breast.

Amanda shuddered exactly as she had done that night.
'No,' she said to herself aloud. But it was too late. She
could feel her clitoris throbbing. She shifted her bottom and
felt a silky wetness spreading over her labia.

She picked up the booklet again and turned the page to
escape the AC/DC woman.

Beautiful brunette looking for single women for sexy times.
You don't have to be experienced. Come here and let me
seduce you. 76 52 89.

Amanda turned that page quickly too, deliberately not
looking at the picture above the ad.

Girl, coffee-coloured, seeks woman to share a passion for
sex. Large breasts and buttocks preferred. If you have
a big, buxom body let me pamper you with pleasure.
31 11 76.

The picture was of a dark-complexioned girl standing
sideways to the camera, her mop of black hair covering
every detail of her face but for the very tip of her nose. She
had petite breasts crested by large nipples and her hand was
stroking the wiry black hair that covered her pubis. She had
long legs and a pert bottom.

Amanda turned yet another page. This time it was the
photograph that caught her eye. It was of a tall, frizzy-haired
blonde. For once her whole face was in the photograph but
with a white triangle plastered over the eyes and nose to
protect her anonymity. She had a large mouth which was
grinning to reveal very white teeth. She was naked but for a
thin, grey-looking suspender belt supporting black stockings
and a pair of black panties. Her legs were wide open and she
was leaning back against a sofa so the gusset of the panties
stretched to cover the whole width of her sex. A few wisps of
blonde pubic hair escaped the panties at the sides and Amanda

could see the distinct hollows in her thighs immediately under her labia. The girl's breasts were heavy but she had small, puckered nipples. Her husband stood behind her in a pair of black G-string pants. Underneath them the outline of his penis was erect.

Young couple. Experienced advertisers looking for females who are willing to try the ultimate. Inexperienced first timers are welcome. We have introduced many to consummate pleasure. You will not regret calling us if you are in need of satisfaction. Must be prepared for AC/DC 07 13 12.

Amanda read the advertisement twice. *Must be prepared for AC/DC.* The words reverberated in her mind. *Must be prepared for AC/DC.* Must be prepared to kiss and stroke and caress a woman. Must be prepared to feel a woman's breasts – the large breasts of the woman featured in the photograph – pressing into her own. Must be prepared to touch a woman's sex, to part her labia and find her clitoris, and to finger it in the way only a woman knows how. Must be prepared to plunge her fingers into the sticky wet pit that was her vagina and feel again the silky velvet walls clenching around them.

Unconsciously Amanda's hand had worked its way under the towel, and up between her legs as she squeezed her thighs together to put pressure on her clit.

'No,' she said aloud, tossing the magazine aside. But it landed on the bed beside her and fell open at exactly the same page, the large mouth of the woman grinning up at her.

Must be prepared to take hold of my black panties and pull them down over my thighs while my husband watches.

'Blast,' Amanda said pulling the towel away from her body.

She did not masturbate that often these days. Oddly, perhaps, she had masturbated most when her sex life with Greg had been at its peak. In the beginning he could make her come exquisitely three or four times, while he held off himself, finally shooting into her or over her with an endless stream of spunk. This experience was so exciting that she would find herself wet the next day, and have to go upstairs to relieve the sexual tension by her own hand. But with the death of their sex life, her desire to masturbate had died too and she couldn't remember the last time she'd played with herself.

Like most women, she supposed, she had a set routine, a ritual she followed invariably. It always started by spreading her legs wide apart and thrusting two fingers, then three as deep into her sex as they would go, cramming them in until her fingers hurt and her labia were strained to the limit. And that is what she did now, sliding down on the bed and stretching across it.

She was not surprised to find herself wet. It was a sticky wetness, like liquid honey. As she pushed her fingers up into her body, she used her other hand to find her clit, stroking gently, the brutality of one hand in contrast to the delicacy of the other. Her clit was already swollen. She brushed it with her finger, dragging it ever so slightly to one side, the feather-like touch making her body shudder.

'Oh, that's so good,' she said aloud.

She turned her head to look at the frizzy blonde, imagining what it would be like to feel her naked body pressing into her own, and that big, fleshy mouth opening for her as they kissed.

She thought of Monica. She remembered the way the woman had slowly kissed her neck, working down to her breasts, as her hand freed them from her blouse and her bra. The shock of her lips fastening on her nipple had been extreme. She was sure it had made her come. Just the feeling of her lips and the touch of her tongue. She'd come again as the woman's mouth had moved lower, as her tongue had parted her labia, and its heat and wetness had caressed her sex.

And she was coming now. Hotly. Hard. Waves of throbbing

pleasure pulsing through her with nothing to hold them back.

'Oh God, this is wonderful,' she moaned, as her first orgasm swelled into a second, one crescendo immediately giving way to another. She was completely out of control, only able to respond to the resonances the photographs and ads had stirred so effectively in her memory.

'Darling, I'm home.'

She hadn't heard the car or the front door opening. She shot bolt upright and scrambled the magazine under the bed.

'Got back earlier than I thought. Where are you?'

She heard Greg's footsteps going into the kitchen. Her face was flushed and she was sure the whole bedroom was redolent of the strong aroma of sex.

'Just taking a shower,' she shouted, grabbing the towel and reaching for her scent. A quick spray gave the room the smell of summer flowers. Amanda dashed into the bathroom and stood under the shower for the second time that evening.

Chapter Two

Amanda let herself into Maggie O'Keefe's house. Maggie had given her a key months ago when she'd asked her friend to take delivery of a new sofa for her. After that Maggie had suggested she should keep the key in case of meter readers, parcel post and emergencies.

Well, Amanda thought, this *was* an emergency of sorts.

Not that she had any intention of deceiving Maggie. Tonight she would tell her what she'd done. She supposed she could have waited till tomorrow and talked it over with Maggie first, but she didn't want to wait now her mind was made up. She had always been impatient.

Maggie's house was untidy. She kept the front room neat and reasonably respectable but the rest of the house, though clean, was a mess. Discarded newspapers and magazines were piled on a chair in the kitchen, boxes and carrier bags from department stores, cooking gadgets, jars and bottles of food and drink mixed with items of make-up littered every surface. Drying washing hung from every available promontory.

Amanda used the phone on the kitchen wall. She had brought *Contacts* with her opened at the ad she had spent most of the morning selecting. She had gone through all the pages carefully but had decided on the one that had specially mentioned 'first timers'. She didn't want to have to pretend that she had done this sort of thing before, that she was more sophisticated than she in fact was. If she was going to go through with this at all – and that was very much a question that remained to be seen – she wanted to be herself.

21

The fact that she found the frizzy haired blonde with the large mouth undeniably attractive was another factor in making her decision, of course. She'd decided on a couple rather than one of the single men because that gave her more options. If she were going to have a sexual fling, she reasoned, she might as well go the whole hog. Having sex with a strong, rampant man would certainly get rid of her frustrations, but the presence of a woman added another dimension to the experience and one, she had to admit, that aroused her profoundly.

So profoundly she'd dreamt about it last night. She had found it hard to settle and when she had finally got to sleep she had a graphic and vivid dream. She had been lying in bed, unable to sleep when the doorbell had rung. Greg woke up and insisted she went down to answer it, saying he was too tired and rolling over and going back to sleep.

Wearily, Amanda had got out of bed. When she got downstairs she realised she was wearing a black lurex body and little high-heeled slippers. That was odd, she thought, because she couldn't remember ever having bought either of them. But what was worse was the body had been cut away to reveal her breasts. It also had no crotch.

The doorbell rang again just as she was going back upstairs to put something decent on. Not wanting to wake Greg again she decided she would have to answer it. There was a couple standing on her front step. Like her the woman was wearing a black lurex body. It had the same cutouts but the woman's breasts were much bigger than hers and she had a thick bush of black pubic hair. Her husband – somehow Amanda *knew* they were married – was fully dressed in a lounge suit, with a very bright yellow tie. He told Amanda that the car was waiting.

Amanda didn't question them. She saw a large car waiting at the end of the path. Then she was in the back seat. She had never seen such a large interior. The carpet was thick and the vast back seat was upholstered in velour. The woman was telling her how strange it was that they were wearing the same outfit. 'You must have known we were coming,' she said. And Amanda realised that she *had* known and that was why she'd put the body on.

The woman began touching Amanda's breasts. It felt nice. She told her to lay back across the seat and open her legs. Her husband was in the front of the car leaning round to watch and it was only then that Amanda realised the car was being driven by a chauffeur. She could see the back of his head and the grey cap he was wearing.

The woman began kissing Amanda's breasts, sucking quite hard on her nipple. Her husband was watching everything and encouraging her to go further. Not that she needed much encouragement. Soon her mouth was pressed firmly to Amanda's sex. She had a long, hot tongue and it was pushing up into Amanda's vagina, just as if it were a small penis.

Amanda was wriggling around. A shock of pleasure closed her eyes and when she opened them again the husband was straddling her chest, his large phallus inches from her lips.

Then the car stopped and as she sucked the husband's cock into her mouth the chauffeur got out of the car and opened the rear door. 'Are you having a good time?' she said as she leant in, pulling her cap off. The chauffeur was Maggie O'Keefe.

Now, in Maggie's house, Amanda decided that she would make a single call on the 'voice mail' system and listen to the message the couple had left. Whether she left a message herself was another matter. It was a question of taking one step at a time.

She dialled the number feeling like a schoolgirl about to go on her first date. Her heart was pounding and she felt breathless.

The phone was answered on the second ring: 'You are connected to the *Contacts Magazine* voice mail system. You may listen to the message left by the advertiser of your choice by keying in the voice mail number appearing at the end of the advert. After you have heard the message you will hear a single tone and you may then leave your own message for them. Thank you for using *Contacts* voice mail service. Have a good day and key in your numbers now.' The voice was female, crisp and precise.

Amanda punched in the six number code. She heard a loud bleep and then a soft woman's voice: 'Hi. My name is Annie Bewley. Thanks for ringing. You've seen our pictures in the ad so you know what we both look like. As we said, we are a married couple who enjoy unconventional sex, especially with another female. If you rang because this is your first time, we really are very *sympatico*, and would be very happy just to meet up for a drink and talk before any commitment. We have a lot of fun in bed and a lot of pleasure and we enjoy sharing and showing others what a good time can be had in the right environment. I am into women but I'm not some aggressive dyke. I love to feel and touch and caress another woman, gently and lovingly. I just happen to find a woman's body a very beautiful thing. So, if what I've said is sort of what you were expecting and if you would like to come along and have a chat with us with a view to starting a little experiment, then leave your message after the tone and don't forget to leave a telephone number where we can contact you. It would be good if you could tell us what you look like. Goodbye for now.'

There was a pause. Amanda hadn't the slightest idea what she was going to do. But as the tone sounded, almost to her own surprise, she found herself saying, 'Oh, hi, ah . . . ah . . . I'm, I mean my name is Mandy. I'm not sure what to say. I've never done anything like this before. Never. But, well . . . It doesn't really matter why, does it? But you do sound nice. I'm not sure if I could go through with it, if you want the truth, but I think I'd like to meet just for a chat like you suggest. I'm blonde, with a slim figure, well I think so, and my friends say I'm attractive. You can call me between eleven and twelve tomorrow on 0181 766 3321. Ah . . . well that's it. I hope I hear from you.' Amanda put the phone down. She wasn't at all sure whether her last remark was true.

*　　*　　*

At ten past eleven the next day Maggie's phone rang. Amanda was sitting in Maggie's front room reading Maggie's copy of *The Independent*. She had told Maggie what she'd done and her friend had been delighted. It was time, she told her, to get on with her life.

The phone startled her. It started her heart pumping.

She got to her feet and went over to the occasional table in the corner where the telephone sat.

'Hello.'

'Is that Mandy?'

She recognised the voice immediately. 'Yes.'

'Hi, it's Annie. You left a message on our voice mail box.'

'That's right.'

'Well, it's nice to talk to you. You sounded very sympathetic.'

'Did you get lots of replies?'

'Lots. But we thought you sounded genuine. You get so many time wasters.'

'What do you mean?'

'Oh, women who get off talking dirty into a phone. You'd be surprised. It's sometimes difficult to sort out the ones who are really looking for a new experience from those who are just doing it to turn themselves on.'

'I had no idea.'

'Why should you? We didn't have any doubts about you, though. This *is* your first time, right?'

'Yes.'

'And, what, you're married?'

'How did you know that?'

'A good guess. A lot of women find that perhaps their sex life is going dull on them. They start looking around for something else.'

'Is that what you did?'

'No, actually it isn't. Phil, that's my husband, and I, we always had a very liberated attitude to sex. Unconventional.

He knew I liked men but I needed women too. We worked out a way to accommodate both our needs. It works very well because we're honest with each other. But some people aren't so lucky.'

'I just don't think my husband is very interested in sex any more.'

'And you are?'

'I think so. I miss it. I miss it a lot. And.' She stopped. What she was about to say was something she'd never told anyone before.

'And you also have certain, let us say, leanings, that refuse to go away,' Annie said.

Annie had made it easy for her. 'I thought I'd forgotten about them until recently.'

'I know. Sex is like that. You can shunt it aside for quite a long time, but then the old needs get stirred up. Presumably you've been with a woman before.'

'Only once.'

'But it excited you?'

'Oh, yes.' Amanda felt sweat breaking out on her forehead. Her palms were getting damp.

'Good. Was that a long time ago?'

'When I'd just left school.'

'How lovely. It would be so nice to introduce you to it all again. I'd love that, I really would.'

'You said we could just talk first.'

'Of course. Of course we can. We wouldn't want to do anything you're not one hundred per cent convinced about. That's the point. You won't have any fun unless you really want to do it.'

'I suppose not.'

'What would be best is if you could come over to us one evening after work. We could have a relaxing drink and talk all you want. No pressure. No commitment. If you don't like us you can just walk away. No hard feelings. Similarly if we don't like you . . .' she left the sentence unfinished.

'That sounds like a good idea,' Amanda said. And she found that was entirely true.

'We're in Chiswick. Where do you live?'

'Islington.'

'No time like the present. Why don't you come on over tonight? Say about seven-thirty. Before you starting getting cold feet.'

'What makes you think I'll get cold feet?'

'It's natural enough.'

She would have to think of an excuse for Greg. 'Fine,' Amanda said more decisively than she felt.

Annie gave her the address and she scribbled it on top of the newspaper.

'See you, then. And don't worry,' Annie said. 'It's just for a drink and a chat.'

'I'll be there.'

As she put the phone down Amanda felt decidedly weak at the knees. She went back to the sofa and sat down. She'd brought *Contacts* with her. She opened it and found Annie Bewley's photograph, staring at the semi-naked woman she had just spoken to. Annie's voice had had a peculiar effect on her. She wasn't at all sure what she had been expecting but she supposed it was someone altogether brasher and more forthright. Annie's approach had been calming. At the same time she had found her voice exciting and couldn't help imagining, as she looked at her half hidden face in the picture, how it would sound mouthing more intimate phrases. The thought made her shudder.

With a distinct effort to pull herself together, Amanda got to her feet. She looked at her watch. To be in Chiswick by seven-thirty she would have to leave Islington no later than six-thirty which meant that Greg would not be back from the office. She would have to phone him to make her excuses.

As she marched down Maggie's hallway and out of the front door, carefully double-locking it behind her, she began to think of what she was going to say.

Back in her own kitchen she poured herself a large mug of steaming black coffee from the electric coffee maker she habitually kept on all morning before picking up the phone.

'Greg Landseer, please,' she said.

'May I ask who's calling?'

'His wife.'

There was a loud click.

'Hi, darling,' Greg said.

'Hi, sweetheart. How's it going?'

'Great. You?'

'Fine. I just thought I'd better let you know I won't be home when you get back.'

'Right.' He didn't sound very interested.

'Janey's invited me over.'

'Oh.'

She knew Greg didn't like Janey. She was a friend she used to work with who was large and garrulous. There was no chance he'd want to come with her, or even ask if she wanted him to pick her up.

'Man trouble again,' she added.

'I'm not surprised. It astonishes me how any man would want to go out with her in the first place.'

'I know. But she's a friend. Do you want me to leave you something to eat?'

'What time will you be home?'

'Don't know.' That at least was true. 'You know how she can talk.'

'I'll get something in the pub.'

'OK. See you later, then.'

'Bye, sweetie.'

It was as easy as that. Amanda sipped her coffee. She had never lied to her husband before, at least not about anything major like going to meet a couple with a view to having sex with both of them at the same time. Since talking to Maggie the day before yesterday everything had happened so quickly. But she hadn't the slightest inclination to put on the brakes.

She was glad that, for once, her life was back on a rollercoaster, as it had been when she first met Greg.

She went upstairs. In the bedroom was a large chest of drawers. She opened the bottom drawer and riffled through the contents. In an effort to put life back into their flagging sex life, Amanda had bought a great deal of exotic lingerie. There was black and red lace, tulle and satin; crotchless panties, white lace basques and tiny G-string panties. She had bras that lifted her breasts into a respectable cleavage and others with no cups at all, her breasts surrounded by a triangle of straps. There were suspender belts as thin as ribbon and others which covered most of her stomach in swathes of pretty lace. When it came to stockings she had every variety and shade of those too, from hold-ups with lace tops to fully fashioned seamed black ones with wide, jet black welts, made from nylon woven with Lycra to give a shiny, high gloss finish.

The question was, which items from this collection should she wear tonight? That was making a very bold assumption of course. Despite what she had said on the phone she found she was assuming the evening would not end in a chat over a bottle of wine. Annie Bewley's attitude, and the sound of her voice, had made Amanda feel confident that she would have the courage of her newly acquired convictions. And that meant she wanted to be suitably prepared.

She sat on the bed and stared into the tangle of satin and lace in the drawer. She always put the stoppers from used scent bottles in with her underwear and the aroma they imparted wafted out at her. If only Greg had been inspired by all this, if only the sight of her dressed in the tight black satin waspie with its long suspenders snaking over her thighs to the black stockings they pulled tautly into peaks had created more than a fleeting interest, she would not have had to look elsewhere.

But they hadn't and that was that. As Maggie O'Keefe had said, if she wanted sex, if she wanted the sort of sex she had

had with Greg in their first months together, she would have to accept that she was not going to get it from her husband, whatever she wore or didn't wear.

She picked out a light blue satin body. It was sexy without being obvious. Quickly she stripped off the maroon tracksuit she wore about the house, took off her bra and panties and slid the satin up her long legs. It clung to her, emphasising the narrowness of her waist and the flare of her hips. The gusset of the garment was so narrow it only covered her labia and revealed the flesh on either side. The legs of the body were cut so high they rested on her hips, exposing the creases of her pelvis.

She sat on the bed again and pulled on a pair of champagne-coloured hold-ups. Again, she thought, black was too obvious. She didn't want to give the impression she was a tart, not yet at least. Smoothing the stockings up over her long legs, she stood up and found a pair of black high heels in the wardrobe.

Amanda examined herself in the full-length mirror mounted on the back of the bedroom door. She turned this way and that. The legs of the body cut diagonally across her firm buttocks. The tops of the stockings were so high they almost brushed her sex. The lingerie made a statement and she decided it was exactly the statement she wanted to make. If this evening ended in polite conversation and cold feet, that was one thing. But if it didn't, they would see that she wasn't entirely naive.

Of course, there was still the question of what dress she should wear. She looked through her wardrobe. There was a high-necked black dress with a knee length skirt and large white buttons that fitted the bill. She got it out and held it up against herself. Yes, that was perfect. It had the advantage of buttoning at the front too, she thought, grinning wickedly before she chastised herself for such wantonness.

The rest of the day passed slowly. She ordered a taxi to pick her up at six-thirty and considered calling Maggie to tell her what had happened. She decided against it. She wasn't sure how she was going to explain to her friend that she'd selected a couple instead of a single man. Since she'd never told Maggie about Monica she wasn't at all sure what she'd say if she decided to let Annie Bewley re-create that experience for her.

In the afternoon she had a long bath and washed her hair. She put on slightly heavier make-up than she usually wore, emphasising her blue eyes with a dark line under her eyelashes, and her cheeks with a hint of blusher. At five she shimmied into the satin body for the second time that day, and pulled on the hold-ups, making sure they were tight and wrinkle free. She brushed out her hair, then put on the black dress, wondering under what circumstances she would be taking it off again.

The last hour passed with agonising slowness. She had tucked her copy of *Contacts* inside a cookery book – a place Greg was sure never to find it – and she refrained from getting it out again to look at Annie and Phil's photograph. Instead she sat in her front room and tried to watch the television, but the afternoon shows on Channel Four were no distraction from the thoughts that whirled around in her head. By six she had convinced herself that the whole thing was a terrible mistake and she should call and cancel the minicab. But she didn't. Something stopped her.

The cab was on time. She set the burglar alarm and double-locked the front door, then settled into the back seat of a Ford Sierra. Fortunately the driver did not appear to have the slightest inclination to talk to her and she sat in silence, gazing out of the window, trying not to think about where she was going and why.

Traffic was surprisingly light, but it still took over an hour to weave through the rush-hour laden streets of Euston, Marylebone, Shepherd's Bush, Parsons Green and Chiswick. It was seven-thirty-five when the car turned into a small, leafy road of identical Victorian houses, two-up, two-down houses with bay windows at the front and a back addition to the rear.

Amanda got the driver to stop six or seven houses before number eighteen. She paid him off and climbed out, straightening her skirt and running her fingers through her hair.

As the car drove off, Amanda walked down the road. Number eighteen had no distinguishing features. Heavy curtains were drawn across the first floor window but the bay window at the front was unobstructed and Amanda could see inside to a small neat room with a fireplace and rows of bookshelves either side of it. The two sofas that faced each other in the middle of the room were empty.

Her heart was pounding so much she could hear it in her ears as she took a deep breath and strode up the very short path to the front door. The door was panelled with frosted glass. On the doorjamb to the right was an illuminated bellpush. Amanda pressed it and was startled by the loud response. She thought she heard whispered voices, then footsteps. A shadow appeared behind the glass.

'Welcome,' Annie said as she opened the door.

'Hi,' Amanda said huskily, finding it hard to breath properly.

'Come in.'

Annie was in her early thirties and much more beautiful than her photograph had suggested. The white triangle that had covered her face had veiled emerald eyes which shone with an expression of amusement and an interest in life that made them impossible to ignore. Her large mouth was symmetrical and pursed, her lips fleshy. She had a tanned complexion and high, sharp cheekbones which were complemented by well-applied make-up and quite heavy eyeshadow.

She directed Amanda into the front room as she closed the front door.

'Would you like a drink? Wine?'

'Red, if you have it,' Amanda said. The front room was empty. There was a bottle of red and a bottle of white wine on a side table and three glasses.

Annie poured the wine.

'Terrible, isn't it, being nervous? It really is like butterflies.

Hundreds of butterflies fluttering in your stomach. Sit down, please.'

Amanda sat down on one of the sofas, and Annie sat opposite. She was wearing a red silk blouse and a pleated black skirt. Her legs were sheathed in very sheer grey nylon and she wore spiky black high heels, the heel itself covered in a metallic finish that gave the impression of highly polished silver. She crossed her legs and the nylon rasped.

'Well,' she said. 'Where do we begin?' She smiled, those very regular white teeth making a spectacular appearance.

'I've never done anything like this,' Amanda said. At that moment she couldn't for the life of her remember why she had thought this would be a good idea. She sipped her wine. 'It's a bit like going to a new dentist.'

Annie laughed. It was a lovely, warm sound 'I know. It's awful. That's the funny thing about sex. We have this convention that everything to do with it is hidden away. I mean people don't just come out and say they want to go to bed with you. That's taboo. Especially for women.'

Amanda thought of Maggie. 'I've got a friend who does.'

'That's great. If you ask me, that's how it should be. We're living in the twentieth century for God's sake. But when it comes to sex most people are still in the fifteenth. There's a mystique about it, like religion, and it's ritualised and made secret. I wish everyone could just be honest and say what they feel, but even when you're brave enough to do that, like you have, your mind's telling you there's something wrong with that and you get all twisted up with nerves.'

'Is that what it is?'

'That's my theory,' Annie said, smiling again.

'I suppose you're right. I've never been very forthright when it came to sex.'

'Until now.'

'Exactly.' Amanda was already feeling better. The conversation had relaxed her. She found herself looking at Annie's legs. They were long and slim, with narrow, pinched ankles.

She remembered what they looked like in the photograph and felt a little thrill of excitement. 'You're a very beautiful woman,' she found herself saying.

'Thank you. I'm delighted you think so. I think you're really lovely too. My husband's upstairs by the way. He'll be down in a minute.'

'Do you do this a lot?'

'You see, that's what I mean. My natural inclination is to prevaricate. Hide things away. Even I haven't broken the habit. But the truth is that we do. We've always really loved sex. We both need it. This way we can keep our marital sex fresh and alive and still continue to please each other as much and as frequently as we did in the beginning. And there's no lying, no clandestine affairs. We do everything openly in front of each other.'

Amanda saw that Annie was looking straight into her eyes as if trying to see what lay behind them.

'How does it work?'

'Originally it was just a question of suggesting to one or two or my girlfriends that they might like to share Phil. I told you I was never an out-and-out dyke. But I always had women, I mean had sex with women. I didn't prefer it to men. It was just wonderfully different. The idea of having both at the same time was really exciting. As most of the girls I was interested in were bisexual, two or three agreed. Then one of them got married and we suggested she brought along her husband.'

'And *Contacts*?'

'It seemed like a good way to get in touch with people who felt the same way we did. What about you? How did you come to be flicking through its advertisements? What made you do that?'

'My neighbour. The woman I just mentioned. She's single. She likes a lot of sex. She's very forthright.'

'Good for her.'

'She gave me a copy. I have to say I never realised such things existed.'

34

'And?'

'I need something.'

'Something?' Annie arched a rather thick eyebrow.

'You're right. Equivocation. I need sex.'

'But you chose an ad that specifically mentioned having sex with a woman.'

Amanda felt herself blush. It was one thing telling the woman about that over the phone; quite another doing it face to face.

'It's all right, you know,' Annie said quietly. 'There's nothing to feel embarrassed about. It's perfectly normal.'

'Is it?'

'Of course. What's so wrong with sharing pleasure with another woman?'

'It's not that I've really missed it, until recently at least. I love men. My husband's a really great lover. But these days he's just not interested and funnily enough . . .' Amanda hesitated.

'Go on,' Annie encouraged.

'It's like they say: nature abhors a vacuum. The less sex I get the more I seem to think about the past.'

'When you had sex with women?'

'Yes. Only one. I only ever did it with one. I was scared after that.'

'Scared of what?'

'Scared of turning into a lesbian I suppose. I didn't want that.'

Annie was grinning. 'What, masculine suits and lace up shoes and short hair combed with a parting?'

'Exactly.' Amanda was smiling too. In Annie's presence the idea seemed absurd.

'And now?'

'Now I suppose I know better. I'd like to experiment. That's why I'm here.'

'Did you answer any other ads?'

'No.'

'Why ours, then?'

'You said you didn't mind someone with no experience. I didn't want to pretend I'm very sophisticated about all this.'

'More wine?' Annie had spotted that Amanda's large glass was already empty.

Amanda nodded and Annie refilled her glass, then sat down again, this time curling her legs up underneath her. 'Here's to experiments,' she said, raising her glass.

They sipped the wine together.

'What happens now?' Amanda asked, her apprehensions melting like mist in the sun of Annie's smile. She had thought the woman beautiful from the moment she had set eyes on her. Now she was beginning to feel strongly attracted to her too.

'Nothing, unless you want it to.'

'And if I do want it to?'

'Some of the women who've replied to the ad have had no experience with other women at all. Can you believe that? But they've got something buried inside them that they need to express. Thinking about it and actually doing it is a big hurdle to jump. You've got the advantage over them because at least you've known what it was like. But it's some time ago, right? So there's still quite a big hurdle.'

That was true. Talking about it in the way they had was quite different from letting Annie take her upstairs. 'It is.'

'What I think you should do, I mean now you've seen me and seen the environs, I think you should try to imagine what it would be like if you came over here and sat down beside me and ever so lightly brushed your lips against mine.'

The words made Amanda's heart start to beat rapidly again.

'Imagine it. Picture it. Can you do that?'

Amanda looked at the woman. Her eyes calculated the distances between the two sofas. Two steps. No more than three. Three steps then turn to sit next to her. No, three steps then kneel up on the sofa and lean forward so their mouths were facing each other. Then brush her lips across that fleshy mouth. Would she use her tongue? Would their breasts be squashed together? She could see the jutting outline of Annie's breast under the blouse.

'Imagine letting your hand fall onto my bosom,' Annie said as if following Amanda's eyes. 'Then kissing me a little bit harder, maybe putting your tongue between my lips. Can you do that?'

'Yes,' Amanda breathed. Her eyes fell to Annie's legs. The skirt had bunched up under her and she could see a good deal of her thighs. Was it her fervent imagination or could she see the barest hint of a stocking top too?

'I'm happy to talk for as long as you want,' Annie said almost in a whisper. 'But if you can imagine doing what I've just described and the thought doesn't repel you, then perhaps we don't need to talk any more.'

Amanda stared at Annie intently. The big smile had disappeared from her face and she was serious, her dark green eyes expressing unmistakable desire. It was that look, more than anything else, that made Amanda's sex pulse powerfully.

'You want me, don't you?' she said.

'Yes. I want to lick you, Mandy. I want to spread your legs open and lick your pussy. I want to put my fingers into you. Then I want to kiss you, let you taste your own juices on my mouth.' Annie had done this many times before. She knew there was a time when she had to tread extremely carefully so as not to scare the woman off, and a moment when a bold statement paid dividends. She sensed the time was right for Amanda to respond to the latter.

'I think I'd like that too,' Amanda said slowly.

'That's very good,' Annie said. 'But it's up to you. If you want to have me you have to come over here. That's a rule of mine. You've got to take the first step, Mandy.'

Amanda got to her feet. She crossed the great divide between the two sofas in three steps, just as she'd imagined she would, and knelt on the seat beside Annie. Exactly as she'd seen it in her mind's eyes she leant forward until their mouths were no more than a couple of inches apart. She had not imagined inhaling the woman's strong, musky scent. It was intoxicating.

Annie did not move. She remained completely passive. It would have been easy for her to raise her head slightly and make contact with Amanda's mouth, but she did nothing. As a sign of her commitment she wanted Amanda to be the one to make the first move.

'Well?' she said quizzically.

Amanda moved forward. Her lips brushed Annie's lips, her tongue darting out for the briefest of touches. Her lips felt hot and soft. She kissed them harder, using her tongue to explore between them. It came up against Annie's and the contact gave her a thrill of pleasure. For a moment their tongues danced against each other until Annie's withdrew and allowed Amanda's dominion over her mouth.

Suddenly Amanda felt a wave of passion. It knocked her reservations aside. She screwed her mouth down onto Annie's and dropped her hand to her breasts. Under the silk blouse she could feel the lace of a bra. She groped around until she found her nipple then rolled it between her fingers, feeling her own nipples react as though she were touching them too.

Eventually Annie broke the kiss. 'That was nice,' she said.

'Yes, it was. You feel so different.'

'Different?'

'Different from a man. Softer. More subtle.'

'Is it like you remember?'

'Yes.'

'As exciting?'

'Definitely.'

'It's all up to you, Amanda. If you want to go home now and think about it, that's all right.'

That was one thing Amanda did not want to do. 'No. No I don't. I want more.'

'Are you sure?'

'Yes.' She said it without the slightest hesitation.

'Then perhaps it's time you met my husband. The thing is we have a rule. It's the only one really. Sometimes one of the girls doesn't want to have a man, they just want to experiment with a woman. Other times they just want a man. That's fine with us. But the rule is we watch each other. That way it's like we're having sex together. We both can share the other's enjoyment. I know it sounds crazy but then it doesn't feel like we've been unfaithful. Can you understand that?'

'Yes. It makes sense. So when do I meet him?'

'If you want to stay, if you want to take it further, you can meet him now.'

'I want to stay.' At that particular moment, with her body still trembling with feeling, Amanda could never remember wanting anything more in her whole life.

Annie took her hand. 'I'm very glad you do,' she said. 'Come upstairs. He's in the bedroom.'

Chapter Three

The bedroom, like the rest of the house, was small. It was papered with a tiny flower print and had a bright blue carpet. The king-size bed was too big for the room and there was no room for any other furniture apart from two small chests of drawers on either side of the headboard.

Heavy, dark blue curtains were drawn across the window and the room was lit by a single bedside lamp that had been dimmed to a pleasant glow. To the left side of the bed was a door which led to a small, white-tiled bathroom.

'Phil, this is Amanda. I've been calling her Mandy but I'm not sure whether she likes that.'

'I prefer it,' Amanda said, looking at the man who was sitting on the edge of the bed. He had a slight figure, with curly brown hair and a pleasant, rounded face.

'Very pleased to meet you, Mandy,' he said standing up and shaking her hand for all the world as if he were just about to sell her an insurance policy.

'It appears,' his wife said, 'that Mandy and I share certain interests.'

'Really? That's good,' Phil said. He was wearing a white shirt and navy slacks. Amanda noticed his feet were bare. 'You didn't break the rules,' he said to his wife without taking his eyes off Amanda.

'He's only asking me that because you're so attractive. Thinks I might have been tempted to seduce you. But I didn't did I? Tell him. He won't believe me. Tell him I forced you to make all the running.'

'She did,' Amanda said.

'Mandy's only ever been with one woman before and that was some time ago.'

'Oh, you mustn't worry. Annie's very gentle,' the man said like a doctor telling a patient the treatment wasn't going to hurt.

'Very,' Annie said with emphasis.

'Did she explain our little pact?' he asked.

'Yes.'

'Good.'

Downstairs her desire to make love to Annie had been overwhelming. If she thought that the injection of her husband into the scenario might have cooled her ardour somewhat, Amanda found she was wrong. In fact it not only seemed to increase her excitement, it made her want to take the initiative again, wanting to show them both she was quite capable of asserting her own desires.

'Shall I take my clothes off, or are you going to do it for me?' she said boldly, looking at Phil.

'You two just get on with it. Try and pretend I'm not here,' he said.

'Well,' Amanda said, turning to Annie.

'I'd like to kiss you again, first,' Annie said.

Amanda turned and swept the woman into her arms, kissing her forcefully on the mouth as her hands caressed her back. She felt the same surge of pleasure she'd experienced downstairs but this time it was increased by feeling the whole length of the woman's body, all its curves and angles and softness, pressed into her own. She plunged her tongue into her mouth. Over her shoulder she saw Phil scramble over the bed to the far corner, resting his head against the headboard then drawing his knees up towards his chin and circling them with his arms. His eyes were rooted to the two women.

'I have to use the bathroom,' Annie whispered, their lips only a fraction of an inch apart.

Amanda released her and she disappeared through the open door, without closing it behind her.

Slowly Amanda unbuttoned her dress as Phil watched. This was the most outrageous thing she had ever done in her life, breaking every convention and taboo, and yet she felt perfectly calm. She might learn to regret it later, but at the moment she was absolutely committed to what she was doing. Thanks to Annie's straightforward approach she was going into it with her eyes wide open.

'You match the bedroom,' Phil said quietly as the light blue satin came into view.

'Do you like it?' Amanda asked, stripping the dress away.

'Very much. I love satin. You've got a lovely figure.'

'I've got a good waist and hips, but I'd like bigger boobs.' The idea of discussing her figure with a man she had only met two minutes before did not strike her as strange. She was enjoying the way he was looking at her, his eyes roaming her body, dwelling particularly on her stocking tops and the way the satin fitted sleekly against her mons, creasing as it dipped between her legs.

'You're very beautiful,' he said.

'She is, isn't she?' Annie said, coming out of the bathroom. She had stripped off her blouse and shirt and was wearing a white lace bra and white suspender belt to support her sheer grey stockings. She was not wearing panties. Her pubic hair was blonde and curly. She walked up to Amanda and turned her back. 'Undo my bra, darling.'

Amanda found the catch and opened it. Annie turned around, allowing the bra straps to fall down her arms. Then she leant forward, holding the bra cups to her breasts, before pulling them away, intensely aware of the two pair of eyes that waited for the revelation.

Amanda had seen her breasts in the photograph. In real life they seemed larger, their nipples a deep ruby red. Their flesh was marked at the side where the bra straps had dug into them.

'Lovely,' she murmured.

'You can touch,' Annie said.

Tentatively Amanda extended her fingers. How long had it been since she cupped a woman's breast in her hand? She weighed the heavy flesh and felt her clitoris spasm.

'Does that feel good?'

'Yes.'

Annie put her hand out. She touched Amanda's shoulder then let her hand stray down the front of the blue satin until she was rubbing her palm against Amanda's left nipple.

'They're very hard,' this was addressed to her husband.

'She's gorgeous,' he said.

'I think you should take this off, don't you?' Annie said, tugging at the body.

If she had paused to think about it for a moment Amanda would have realised that this was the point of no return. She could easily have put her dress back on and walked out of the room, down the stairs and out of the front door. It would not be difficult to get a cab. She could be back in her own home in an hour none the worse for wear, a kiss and a caress the extent of her infidelity. But she did not care to do any such thing. Instead she slipped the shoulder straps of the body down her arms and wriggled out of the tight-fitting garment.

'Keep the stockings on,' Phil said. 'We both love stockings.'

Amanda let the body drop to the floor. She did not bother to pick it up.

'Now we can relax,' Annie said, sitting on the bed and patting the spot beside her. 'Are you still nervous?'

'No.' It was true. The waves of excitement she felt had banished Amanda's nerves. She sat down.

'Good.'

Annie's hand came around her shoulder and her mouth kissed her on the neck, little sucking kisses that created a rash of goose bumps on her arm. Annie's other hand cupped her breast, her fingers plucking at her nipple.

'When you were with your other lady, did you use a dildo?' she asked softly.

'Yes.' Monica had introduced her to dildoes. She had made her come by holding one in her vagina while she licked her clitoris with her tongue. Amanda remembered the feeling vividly.

'Good.' She delved into the top drawer of the bedside chest and came out with two cream, plastic dildoes of identical size. 'I love that too. Lie back now, let me pleasure you. See if I can arouse all those feelings you had before.'

That was not going to be a problem, Amanda thought. Her body was already hyped up. She lay back on the bed, glancing at Phil as she did so. He was watching everything they did intently, though he had not moved.

'Sometimes,' Annie said, kneeling at Amanda's side. 'I put one of these inside me in the morning and wear a very tight pantie girdle all day to keep it in.'

'By the time I get home she's in a terrible state,' Phil said.

Annie spread her knees apart. Amanda saw her labia. They were pursed and prominent and clearly already wet. She watched as Annie nosed the torpedo-shaped head of the dildo between them and then slid it up into her vagina until only an inch or two of the base was visible. She shuddered. 'Oh, that's lovely.'

Closing her legs to hold the dildo in place she leant forward, and kissed Amanda lightly on the lips. She worked her mouth down over her throat and onto her breasts, kissing each in turn and pinching both nipples between her teeth. Then she licked and sucked and kissed her way down Amanda's stomach while she slipped one hand between her thighs and eased them apart.

As her tongue approached her mons Amanda felt another surge of excitement. She felt her clitoris flex in anticipation.

Two things happened then. She felt the tip of the dildo, cold and hard, nudging between her lower labia as the tip of Annie's tongue, hot and wet by contrast, parted the upper lips of her sex and fastened on her clitoris. As the tongue winkled out the little nut of nerves, the dildo was pressed home, sliding into the soaking wet tube of flesh without the slightest resistance.

The shock made her cry out. As it subsided Amanda turned her head to the side to look at Phil. His eyes were riveted to her belly.

'Is that good?' Annie asked as she held the dildo in the depths of Amanda's sex.

Amanda didn't answer. Instead she wriggled her body down on the big, hard phallus. It was better than good. It was great.

Annie's tongue was back on her clit. It began pushing it from side to side, in a slow rhythmic movement, the same rhythm her hand was using to pull the dildo up and down the tight, wet tube of Amanda's cunt.

'She's good at this,' Phil said.

It was true. The movement was perfect. Amanda felt her body clench, all the precursors of orgasm gathering like clouds on a stormy day. Ripples of pleasure ran between her clit and the velvety interior of her vagina as it clung to the dildo.

'She's making me come,' she told Phil in a whisper.

Suddenly Annie's approach changed. She pushed the dildo up and down more forcefully and ground Amanda's clit back against the underlying bone with her tongue. The head of the dildo pressed right up against the neck of Amanda's womb just as her orgasm broke.

In her mind, as the waves of pure pleasure crashed over her, she saw Monica as vividly as she saw Annie, the two experiences joined in the heat of passion, all the intensity and sensation of the first recreated by the second. It went on a long time. Amanda found, by twisting her hips from side to side, she could move the head of the dildo around inside her, and some instinct told Annie to hold the dildo in place and not withdraw it again.

Eventually the crescendo died away. Amanda sat up. The

image of Monica in her mind had been so vivid that she half expected to see her kneeling on the bed.

'You're very responsive,' Annie said. 'That's exciting.' She took her hand away and the dildo slipped down slightly. But Amanda didn't want that, and scissored her legs together to keep it in place.

'Let me,' Amanda said. She was not sure what she was going to do but she knew she wanted to take the initiative. Wrapping her hand around the back of Annie's neck she pulled her down on top of her and kissed her on the mouth, revelling in the fleshiness of her body as it pressed against hers, and the wonderful softness of her mouth. It was completely different from kissing a man and the difference was terribly arousing.

She squirmed her thigh up between Annie's legs and felt the butt of the dildo protruding from her sex. That gave her an idea.

'Will he help?' she whispered to Annie.

'Whatever you want.' Annie answered.

'Turn them on,' Amanda said looking at Phil. 'Both of them together.'

Phil didn't need to be asked twice. For the first time since the two women had lain down together on the bed he moved, getting up on to his knees beside them. Amanda could see the outline of his large erection tenting his trousers. She felt his hand pushing between her thighs and she opened them to let it in. Suddenly a strong vibration coursed through her belly, as the dildo was pushed deep again. A second later she felt Annie's body begin to tremble too, a loud humming noise filling the air. The vibrations were powerful, the one feeding off and enhancing the other. This was unexplored territory. She had never done anything like this with Monica.

Shifting her position slightly she angled her sex up towards Annie. The breadth of the dildoes held their labia apart, exposing both women's clitoris. Amanda wriggled her hips, shifting her position, trying to get their clits to butt against each other. Suddenly she felt the unmistakable little button of flesh nestling against her own. It was swollen and hard, and she could feel it vibrating exactly as her own was doing, the powerful vibrators affecting every part of their sex. The sensation caused a new shock of pleasure. Annie clearly felt it too as she moaned loudly and reared up, arching her body like a bow so she too was thrusting her sex forward to improve the connection.

Annie was coming. Amanda could feel it. Not only was her whole belly trembling, but her clitoris had began to spasm. In seconds Amanda's own was responding like for like. She was literally wallowing in pleasure, the firm pressure from Phil's hand holding the dildo in place as its vibrations titillated all her most sensitive nerves, the feeling of Annie's big breasts dragging across her chest, and most of all the squirming of their clits against each other, all creating surges of passion.

She opened her mouth to cry out, but Annie covered it with her own, plunging her tongue deep. They clung together as their orgasms exploded, the feeling of one accelerating and emphasising the feeling of the other. Each high was matched and bettered, one climbing over the other as though hand over hand, until finally they reached a peak, every nerve was straining, every sinew stretched.

They were breathless, panting for oxygen, the fire of passion having consumed it all.

'Quite a performance,' Phil said, grinning, 'for a beginner.'

Annie rolled off Amanda. 'You can say that again,' she said, flopping over on to her back, quite exhausted.

But Amanda's reaction was quite different from Annie's. Her orgasm had not left her enervated. Quite the reverse. It had created a need in her quite as strong as anything she had felt earlier.

She sat up, allowing the dildo to slip from her body. 'Is it your turn now?' she asked Phil wantonly, looking straight into his eyes. She didn't wait for a reply. She seized the zip of his fly and pulled it down over the bulge of his erection, then delved inside. She freed his cock and pulled it clear. It was circumcised and large, though the glans was a little smaller in diameter than the shaft that supported it, giving it a pointed appearance.

Not that that worried Amanda. She leant forward and gobbled it into her mouth.

'Well,' Annie said. 'Looks like you're going to get a treat.'

Phil started unbuttoning his shirt. He pulled it off then took Amanda's head in his hands. 'Let me take my stuff off,' he said, easing her back.

Amanda sat up again. She watched as Phil stripped off his trousers and white briefs. She thought this was probably the sexiest experience she had ever had in her life, bar none. After making love with a woman, with all the softness of her body, and the coldness of a dildo inside her, what could be more perfect than to have a man, ready and waiting, with a live phallus, hot and throbbing, ready to plunge into her?

'I'm so turned on,' she said to nobody in particular.

Phil stood by the side of the bed, naked. She had seen his body in the photograph, all but his genitals. Though he was not fat he had little muscle tone. That did not bother her. As he sat back on the bed again she grabbed his arm and pulled him over on top of her, feeling his cock pressing against her belly.

They kissed. His mouth was different to his wife's, more bony and angular. Amanda felt a new wave of arousal. She could have whatever she wanted.

'Kiss me,' she said turning to Annie, who was still lying next to her on the bed.

Annie obliged, her tongue darting into Amanda's mouth where only a few seconds before her husband's had been.

'Lovely,' Amanda said, her body filled with new sensations.

Phil wriggled himself between her legs, his cock parting her labia.

'Yes,' Amanda encouraged, trying to squirm her way down on to it.

But he teased her, pulling away, his hand snaking down over his wife's belly until he felt her pubic hair. She opened her legs for him, knowing what he wanted and he pushed two fingers deep into her vagina.

'Please . . .' Amanda begged.

'I like to hear it,' he said, enjoying the power.

'Please put it up me,' Amanda said, the words exciting her too. She could see his hand screwing itself up into his wife. That was arousing too. She felt her clit respond, twitching wildly.

'Not good enough,' he said, raising himself so he was poised above her, his cock nosing into the mouth of her vagina.

'Give it to me . . .' She struggled to find the words that would satisfy him. 'Put it in my cunt.'

He smiled, a twisted, wicked smile, and fell on her, driving his prick all the way up her until it was completely buried. She could feel his balls slapping against her body.

Immediately he began to pound into her. He was stronger than he looked, his thrusts powerful and regular, reaching to the very top of her vagina.

Amanda felt her sex clinging to him. Her clitoris, hammered by the base of his shaft, was delivering huge ripples of pleasure, each one a stepping stone towards what she knew would be an inevitable climax. She wouldn't be able to hold out for long.

Her eyes had been closed by the impact of his first penetration but she opened them again when she felt Annie's body moving against her. With her husband's fingers still impaled inside her, she turned on her side, pressing her big breasts against both their bodies. Her hand caressed his buttocks then delved down between his legs, groping around until she could gather his scrotum between her fingers.

Amanda felt Phil's reaction. As his wife pulled his balls back, away from him, his cock spasmed violently against the tight confines of Amanda's sex and he moaned, burying his face in Amanda's neck.

'He likes this,' Annie said matter-of-factly.

Her hand ground his scrotum back against Amanda's body then pulled it out again. His cock was jerking so violently she was sure he was going to come and she was certain she was coming too, this new development only serving to fuel the fires of her need.

'You're making me come,' she said, though she was not sure who she meant by that. They both were. Equally.

Suddenly there was something new to cope with. As Phil drove forward his balls were free again, slapping hard against her, but a finger, Annie's finger, was pressing up under his cock. The copious juices Amanda had produced greased its passage. Before she could work out what she was going to do she had done it, plunging her finger into Amanda's vagina alongside her husband's phallus.

'Oh, God,' Amanda moaned, staring at Annie in wonder. She couldn't believe she could take it but she could. Not only that but it was intensely exciting. Her whole sex was spasming, clenching and relaxing, then clenching again, her orgasm blossoming.

But the new invader had the same effect on Phil. His wife's finger sawed up and down the length of his cock, as if massaging the spunk out of it. As he withdrew on the outward stroke it hooked over his glans rubbing the wetness of Amanda's sex into the tender flesh. He simply couldn't take it any longer. He thrust back up one more time, feeling the finger wriggling against him, then came, the spasms of his cock fighting against Amanda's vagina made tighter by being so sorely stretched.

His spunk sputtered out. Amanda could feel it more acutely than she ever had before. She could feel each jet of it not only spattering the walls of her sex but running down Annie's finger, hot and sticky. Then it was her turn to explode. Her eyes closed and her sinews snapped as her body refused to take any more. It was not just the physical sensations, it was what was going on in her mind. She was surrounded by sex, wrapped in it. Everywhere she looked, everything she felt was a function of her sexual pleasure. She arched her head back against the sheet, and hoped the feelings would never die.

But as they did, as she felt Phil's cock soften and Amanda's finger slip from her body, she knew one thing for certain. Sex would never be the same again.

'So?' They sat at Maggie's kitchen table. It was Saturday morning and too early to drink so Maggie had made tea. She always insisted on the real thing, despising tea-bags, and the teapot sat on the table, covered with a tea cosy made from little squares of material like a patchwork quilt.

'So, what?' Amanda said conquettishly.

'Come on, tell Aunty Maggie all. It was my idea.'

'True. Well I went to this house in Chiswick.'

'No. Start from the beginning. You called the voice mail and gave this number. And they called you back.'

'Right. That's all. We had a little chat and the woman said it was all right if I wanted just to go and talk about it. I mean I wasn't obligated to do anything. So I got a cab to their house.'

'And what did she look like?'

'Lovely.'

'And the guy?'

'I didn't meet him at first.'

'So you talked to the woman.'

'Right.'

'And then?'

'There wasn't any, "and then",' Amanda said looking blank. But she could not hold the expression for long and her face broke into a grin.

'Liar.'

'And then we went upstairs. They were really nice, Maggie. Nice is the wrong word. They made me feel . . . secure.'

'What was the guy like?'

'He was slim, not very fit but surprisingly powerful.'

'Powerful. Well that sounds good. And a nice big cock?'

'Maggie!'

'Well, I know it's not the size that counts but what he can do with it.'

'He knew just what to do with it.'

'Great! And did wifey join in?'

'Let's just say she was very co-operative.'

Amanda had thought long and hard about what she was going to tell her friend. As she had never discussed her lesbian experience with her she had decided to skip over the details of what had happened with Annie, and concentrate on what she had done with Phil.

'If you want the truth, I think it was the best time I've ever had in bed.'

'Really?'

'It was fantastic. I mean fantastic. I've never felt so alive.'

'That's great.'

'Of course, I feel terribly guilty about Greg.'

'Oh, come on, he's ignoring you. What are you supposed to do?'

'I don't know. Don't get me wrong. I don't regret it for a second. But it's the lying.'

'It's worth it. I thought we'd agreed it would probably save your marriage. Come on I want all the gory details. What did they do to you?'

Amanda told her, starting from the moment she unzipped Phil's trousers. She told her how Annie had grabbed his balls but edited what she'd done subsequently.

'Sounds like you had a really good time.'

'Aren't you shocked?'

'Should I be? Come on, Mandy, you know I've done most things.'

'Have you been with a couple?'

'Do you want the truth?'

'Of course.'

'I told you I used *Contacts*. Sometimes I've gone to a couple's house just like you did. And since this is true confessions you tell me something. Why did you chose a couple? I thought you'd go for a single man.'

It was the one question Amanda had hoped she wouldn't ask. She thought she might be able to gloss over that. She should have known Maggie would home in on the truth.

'No reason,' Amanda said too quickly. 'I just liked the look of them in the photograph.'

'You're not a very good liar.' Maggie sipped her tea. 'The reason I've done it is simple. I like women. I've never told you this because I thought it might affect our friendship, but I'm into women as well as men.'

Amanda found herself grinning again.

'What's the grin for?' Maggie asked.

'There's something I've never told you too.' The grin relaxed into a smile. Suddenly something she had thought was going to be difficult was easy. Maggie had given her the perfect opening. 'Would it shock you if I said, snap?'

'You sly dog. So you've given me the edited version have you?'

'I had this . . .' She tried to think of the right word, '. . . fling with a woman. Only once. Recently it's sort of haunted me. When you gave me that magazine and I saw the ads, well, I don't know. I just wanted to try it again.'

'It's perfectly all right.'

'I know that now. But I was scared. I don't want to be a lesbian.'

Maggie laughed. 'It's not mutually exclusive.'

'Exactly. So now I know.'

'And what are you going to do about it?'

'I'm going to enjoy myself. As simple as that.'

'Well, in that case . . .'

Maggie got to her feet. She took a photograph from the drawer of the kitchen table and handed it to her friend. 'Adrian and Natasha Chrystal,' she said. 'They're good friends of mine. Give them a ring. I think you'd like them.'

'What sort of friends?'

'The sort we've just been talking about.'

'Really?'

'Yes. I met them through *Contacts*.'

'You've been to bed with them?'

Maggie nodded.

'Why didn't you suggest this before?'

'Because if you remember, dear girl, last time we talked about this you weren't even sure you wanted to take the magazine home with you, let alone ring up a couple and have them take you in turns.'

'I guess I got carried away.' Amanda looked sheepish.

'You certainly did. And a good thing too. If I'd known that's what you wanted to get into I'd have suggested the Chrystals in the first place.'

'And they're into all this?'

'They're rich. They're bored. At least I think that's the explanation. They love sex and they're very imaginative.'

'What does that mean?'

'Go around and see for yourself.'

'Do you think I should?'

'What?'

'Perhaps I should stop while I'm ahead.'

'You've only just started.'

'It really was exciting.'

'How long ago since you had your fling?'

'When I was eighteen. The odd thing was that when Annie was touching me I remembered how it was with Monica – that was her name – I remembered exactly what she did. It was almost like she was there with us.'

'Did you tell Greg about it?'

'I never told anyone until Annie.'

'Annie?'

'The wife.'

'Did it last for long?'

'A couple of weeks. She taught me everything. Then, like I said, I got frightened. Monica was only into women. She understood. At least she said she did. She was very kind to me. But what about you? I had no idea, Maggie, really. Why haven't we ever talked about this before? I mean, you've told me everything else about your sex life.'

'I didn't know how you'd react. I didn't want you to start imagining that whenever we were alone together I was thinking about getting into your knickers.'

Amanda laughed. 'Don't worry, I'll keep my legs crossed from now on.'

'More tea?'

'Please.'

Maggie took the tea cosy off the pot and poured more dark amber liquid into the cups before topping them up with milk.

'So how did you get into it?' Amanda said, wrapping her hands around her mug.

'Oh, I'm not entirely sure. I think in the beginning it was pure curiosity. You know how I love sex. I always have. And I love trying new things. I suppose it was about three years ago, maybe four. I was having this relationship with an airplane pilot. He used to like a lot of verbal, you know, me whispering in his ear what a big cock he had and how I wanted him to shoot his stuff right up me. That sort of thing. The more obscene the better. It turned me on too so I didn't mind.'

'Everything turns you on.'

'Exactly. More importantly, it really got him going. He would really give me a good time. Then he started asking me to say other things.'

'What sort of things?'

'Like describing other men and what they'd done to me. I didn't mind. I gave him long descriptions of all my sexual experiences. It really drove him wild. And that drove me wild. So I started making stuff up. Well, one day, I developed this long scenario about how I'd been with this married man, in bed with him, and his wife had walked in. I told him that instead of being cross she climbed into bed with us and started touching me. So there's this guy pounding into me like crazy, and I'm telling him how this woman was squeezing my tits and putting her hand down between my legs, and I suddenly realise I'm getting really turned on by it. The more detail I make up, the hotter I get. I can still remember it. By the time this imaginary woman and I are doing sixty-nine, my bloke is popping his cork and I'm completely gone. Don't think I've ever had an orgasm like it.'

'And that got you thinking?'

'Right. I'd never imagined being touched by a woman before. Suddenly I couldn't get it out of my head. The next night I went round to this pilot's flat again. We were having a bottle of wine, but in seconds I was telling him how the wife had called me and asked me over. That when I got there she was naked with this big dildo strapped on her hips. She started fucking me with it, I told him. He literally threw me on the floor and fucked me with all our clothes still on. And I was so wet you could have launched the Queen Elizabeth on my slipway.'

'So, what did you do?'

'I thought about it a lot. I bought a girlie magazine. Penthouse or something. I started looking at all these beautiful women and imagining what it would feel like to be in bed with them. It would always end with me masturbating.'

Amanda remembered how looking at *Contacts* had had exactly the same effect on her.

'And?'

'You want all the details?'

'Of course.'

'Well, I decided it wasn't any good just dreaming about it. I thought I should get out there and do something.'

'How?'

'It was easy. I looked up *Time Out's* listings and found a gay

57

bar. I got myself dogged up in a little black skirt and my best tights and high heels. I wore a bra that lifted my tits right up under my chin and squeezed myself into a little halter top that showed off my cleavage and walked into this place. I ordered a gin and tonic and looked around. It was like a sweet shop. I couldn't decide which to have.'

'Maggie!'

'Well, it was true. I couldn't believe it. I always thought of dykes as butch and chunky. There were women in there most men would have died for. Long, willowy types, short brunettes with faces like dolls, intense intellectuals with horn-rim glasses and tweed skirts. And girls who looked like they'd represented East Germany in the shot put.'

'All available?'

'More or less. There were two or three couples but most were in gaggles of five or six. I was only standing at the bar for thirty seconds when this girl came over to me. She was a brunette with long hair practically down to her bum and a very slim body. She was wearing a pink silk dress and white tights and boots. A refugee from the sixties. She asked me if I'd been in the bar before. I said I hadn't done anything before. She bought me a drink.'

'And you went off with her?'

'No. We were talking when two other women came up to her. She introduced me. One of the women was American. She was gorgeous. She was probably forty but didn't look it. She was wearing a St Laurent suit – you know, tailored and businesslike – and an expensive diamond bracelet. She had this lovely hair, a shining auburn, tied up in a French pleat and these long, elegant legs. Her tights were so sheer you could hardly see them.'

'And?'

'She ordered a bottle of champagne. The woman she'd come over with seemed more interested in the brunette than in her, so we started talking. She was in the rag trade, a buyer for one of the big American stores. After a couple of drinks she

58

asked me if I wanted to go to bed with her. Just like that. I said I would like that very much. She dropped a twenty-pound note on the bar to pay for the drinks and we were out of there like greased lightning. She had a car waiting outside. A limo complete with chauffeur.'

'What, on a fashion-buyer's salary?'

'Turns out she wasn't only the buyer. She owned a whole chain of stores. Or her family does. So we were sitting on the back seat and I thought I'd better tell her I'd never done it before. She took that in her stride. She turned and touched my face with her hand, very gently, then kissed me on the lips. Well, they weren't kisses, really. She licked my lips with her tongue, very delicately. It was wonderful. I can still feel it. I don't think I've ever been so excited. I wrapped my hand around her neck and pulled her closer, and there I was kissing a woman for the first time, tongue down her throat, my tits crushed against hers. I could feel her nipples. They were like little chips of ice, hard but cold. That turned me on too for some reason. So did the fact that I could see the chauffeur watching in his rear view mirror. Then she broke away and sat up straight, all prim and proper with her legs crossed, and started talking about her job, as if nothing had happened.'

'And then?' Amanda prompted. Maggie's story was making her feel distinctly hot. She shifted her bottom on the chair, suddenly intensely aware of the gusset of her panties cutting up between her legs. She didn't dare to reach down to try and ease it out with her hand. Half-an-hour ago she wouldn't have been so self-conscious.

'We drove up to this really smart house in Hampstead. Carriage driveway. Video security. The works. When we were inside, she took me into this sitting room the size of Wembley stadium and offered me a glass of champagne. Krug mind you. She asked me if I would excuse her for a couple of minutes, then come up to the bedroom. And off she went.'

'Did you get cold feet?'

'You're joking! I was so excited I swear I wet my knickers.'

'Maggie!'

'It was true! So, after the five minutes, I walked up this big sweeping staircase. There wasn't much doubt which room she was in – there were these double doors at the end of the corridor and one of them was ajar. So I went in and there she was lying on this vast bed, with cream silk sheets and satin pillows like the set of some Hollywood film, and she'd got this fabulous silk satin and lace slip on and nothing else. And that was that.'

'Oh, come on, you can't stop there! Tell me what she did.'

'Use your imagination,' Maggie said, grinning.

'Come on. I told you.'

'Most of it. Well, she asked me to take my clothes off for her. So I stood there and stripped, like I was doing it for a man. I was really getting hot by this time, because she'd started to play with herself while she was watching me. Her pussy was shaved, completely. I couldn't wait to stroke her. When I got to my panties, she got off the bed and started to help me, kneeling at my feet, and pulling them down. Then she kissed my belly and caressed my arse.' Maggie gave a little moan and shuddered, the memory still vivid. 'Well, then we got onto the bed and she kissed me and I kissed her. And I just sort of lost track. It was wonderful. She knew just what to do.'

'And after that?'

'Oh, I saw her a lot. Then she had to go back to America. After that I went back to the club a few times but I never found anyone like her. Then I got into *Contacts*. I found the perfect complement to sex with a man is sex with a woman and vice versa. Simple as that.'

'And the Chrystals?'

Maggie smiled. 'I think you should judge that experience for yourself.'

Chapter Four

Amanda had no problem deciding what she was going to wear this time, because she was convinced the evening would end in bed. She supposed if the Chrystals were physically repulsive, or dirty and unkempt, that she might have second thoughts, but though Maggie had declined to give her any details she could not believe that her friend would sleep with the couple unless they were attractive and personable.

So, working on what she thought was that fair assumption, she had laid out a scarlet red basque and matching, thong-cut panties. She had already had a long bath and taken her time over her make-up, finding a lipstick that matched the scarlet of the lingerie, and now she sat on the edge of the bed, unwrapping a new pair of stockings from their cellophane. She bunched the nylon in her fingers and inserted her toe in the pocket she had created. Slowly, she rolled the sheer and shiny black nylon up her leg, watching as it encased her flesh, clinging to every contour like a second skin.

With the wide, jet black stocking tops banding her thighs, Amanda reached over to the basque and pulled it around her body. The silky material felt cold. It would have puckered her nipples instantly if they hadn't already been as hard as stone. She fastened the long set of hooks and eyes at the back, choosing the tightest of the three positions. The basque was boned and she felt a curious thrill as the garment tightened around her, narrowing her waist and pushing her breasts into a respectable cleavage. Instead of the normal four the basque had six suspenders, each long and thin, the actual clip covered with a diagonal sash of satin. Carefully, Amanda adjusted the suspenders to hold the stockings tautly. She had to stand up to secure the last two as they were positioned at the back and cut down across her buttocks.

She stepped into the panties and drew them up her legs. They rasped against the nylon of the stockings. As they settled between her legs she felt a little frisson of pleasure. Not surprisingly, her labia seemed to have become sensitised. Since her evening with Phil and Annie she had spent most of her time thinking about sex. And Maggie's revelations hadn't helped. On Sunday, with Greg asleep in front of the television, she had found herself sneaking upstairs and masturbating quickly and furtively in the bathroom with the door locked. Despite the unpromising conditions she had come wildly, jamming a towel in her mouth the stop herself screaming with pleasure.

She had called the Chrystals on Monday morning using her own phone. Natasha Chrystal had already spoken to Maggie, so their conversation was brief. Natasha had given her their address and asked her to come round at seven on Tuesday. Amanda had told Greg she was going to the movies with Maggie, who willingly agreed to cover for her.

There was a time in her relationship with Greg when he had been very interested in her shoes. He loved high heels, he told her, and, always willing to oblige, she had gone to a specialist shop she'd found in King's Cross and bought three pairs of outrageously high-heeled stilettos, in red, white and black patent leather. She'd also bought one pair of red leather ankle boots with lace up fronts, their heel only a slightly more sensible height. She had decided to wear them tonight. Climbing into them, she drew the black laces tight then examined herself in the mirror. She was transformed. The suburban housewife had become a whore, ready to ply her trade on the street. She smiled at herself. Dressed like this she thought she could probably make her fortune.

She had decided on a red dress too. It was jersey and tight, emphasising the hour-glass figure the basque had enhanced, if not created. It showed the lines of the corset under it, of course, and even the little nubs of the suspenders, but as far as Amanda was concerned, the effect was very sexy. She hoped the Chrystals agreed.

The taxi she had ordered arrived at six-thirty. She left a note for Greg and locked up, not bothering with a coat. Though it was only the beginning of April, the weather had been warm for the last three days and the forecast was that it would get warmer still.

The Vauxhall Carlton smelled strongly of the car deodorant hanging from the ash tray in the front. It also smelt of stale cigarettes. As the driver wove his way through the traffic Amanda stared out of the side window, seeing nothing. Five days ago she had been in another taxi but her feelings had been very different. She had felt trepidation as well as excitement. Now, though her heart was very definitely in her mouth, it was entirely due to the thrill of what she was allowing herself to do.

She had no regrets. Though she wished she didn't have to lie to Greg – she didn't like lying – she knew that was the price she had to pay for suddenly being plunged back into the middle of an invigorating sex life. Since it was a price she was prepared to pay, there was no point crying over spilt milk. She liked sex. She needed sex. It was only now, after her shattering experience with Phil and Annie, that she realised precisely how much she needed it. She felt fully alive again, her mind alert, her body tingling with new sensations.

Apparently her husband felt differently. He seemed content with an increasingly rare quickie, often after they'd been out for a meal and he'd had too much to drink. He would turn her on her side, spoon in behind her and slip his not very hard penis into her. It would all be over in a matter of seconds. Usually, she wouldn't know he had come until she felt him slip out of her again, though occasionally he did grunt loudly at the climactic moment. Gone were the days when she would raid the shops for the latest line in lingerie, send for exotic lingerie catalogues advertised in the Sunday papers, and spend hours choosing what to buy. Gone were the days when she dressed, as she was dressed now, like an expensive whore, and they'd spend hours together, fucking until they were sore. Greg barely glanced at her now, whatever she was wearing. When once he had licked every inch of her fetishistic shoes, sucking on the heels before he worked his way along her leg and up to her cunt, now he could barely be bothered to kiss her on the cheek when he got back from work in the evening.

Perhaps that's why she felt no guilt, Amanda thought. Greg didn't seem prepared even to try to get their sex life back on track.

Well, she was not going to settle for celibacy.

She had no idea how this adventure she had embarked on would end. She didn't want to think about that. She was in it for one reason and one reason only. Pleasure. Pure sensual pleasure. What she had experienced in Chiswick had been so extraordinarily blissful she was determined she was going to repeat the experience again. And again. One day, perhaps, she would grow jaded, and begin to tire of it all, as quite clearly her husband had done. Then they would be perfectly matched. Then she could settle for what he had to offer and would not resent his lack of interest in her. That would be in the future. This was now.

Amanda shifted in her seat. The basque held her body in a grip of steel. The third suspender cut across her buttocks awkwardly. It was acutely uncomfortable and, at the very same time, incredibly sexy. She realised she had never worn the corset outside the bedroom. Nor had the ankle boots even seen the light of day. They made her feel louche and wicked.

'Busy are you?' the driver said as they sat in a traffic jam just before the elevated section of the Westway. He was a man of about fifty with a big gut that threatened to burst the buttons of his shirt.

Amanda wasn't sure how to answer so she said nothing.

'Must be,' he replied. 'Must get a lot of calls. I've done quite a few of the girls. See, I only work nights. You're an early bird.'

'Am I?' Amanda took little notice.

'Yeah, most of them it's up to the clubs, or dinner. Never before about ten. Sometimes like midnight. Then I have to wait. I don't mind, I get paid. Do you want me to wait, by the way?'

'No.'

'Too early, see. You're all right early on. Later you get the drunks. Guys on the make. Never know what problems you could run into. More sensible to have me wait. Especially if they've got another job to go to.'

'I suppose so,' Amanda said, not having the faintest idea what he was talking about.

'You know that,' he said.

'Yes,' she agreed for the sake of piece and quiet.

She didn't get it. 'Haven't seen you before though. If you don't mind me saying so you're a real looker.' The traffic moved and the car started forward.

'I don't mind,' she said.

'Makes me feel young again, looking at you,' he said. 'Wish I could afford it.'

'Afford what?' Amanda said puzzled.

'Afford you.'

'I'm sorry?'

'You know, afford a session with you.' He was staring at her in the rear view mirror. The mirror was tilted down and she was sure he was looking at her legs. 'Still, I can dream I suppose. What's it going to cost him? Do you mind me asking? I might want to save up and buy myself a birthday present.'

It was then that the penny dropped. He thought she was a call girl, obviously an expensive one. He'd worked out she was on the way to meet a client. Clearly she wasn't the only one who thought she looked like a tart.

His assumption did not offend her, in fact she was flattered. Rather awkwardly in the confined space in the back of the car, she managed to cross her legs, her skirt riding up her thigh. He might just get a glimpse of her stocking tops, she thought.

'It depends what you want,' she said, trying to hide her grin. 'The works comes expensive.'

'The works?' he said hoarsely.

'Yes. You know, a very slow strip, black stockings, lacy lingerie, then a long massage, every part of your body rubbed in oil. And that's just for starters.'

The man gulped audibly. 'Jesus,' he said. They were heading down the slip road leading to Shepherd's Bush. 'So what does that cost?'

'Five hundred.'

'Worth every penny, I bet.' His eyes studied her face then wandered down to her legs. A bus veered in front of them and he narrowly missed it. Amanda decided she'd better pull her skirt down for her own safety.

They turned into Holland Park and then drove down into Kensington. The Chrystals' house was on the corner of a Georgian stucco-fronted terrace just off Kensington High Street.

'Thanks,' she said to the driver as she got out.

'Have fun,' he said.

'Don't worry, I always do,' she said, giving him an exaggerated wink.

He drove away, his eyes lingering on her as long as he dared as she walked up to the front door. Though the heels of the boots were not as high as the shoes she had bought for her bedroom frolics they were still higher than anything she normally wore and she found she had to take small, diminutive steps.

The front door was stripped and varnished oak. It had a brass door knocker and no bell. The ground floor windows on either side were veiled by lace curtains and Amanda could not see inside.

She rapped the knocker. Her heart had begun to thump against her ribs. She was here for one reason and one reason only. To have sex. The unambiguousness of that fact was immensely exciting.

'Hi.'

The woman who opened the door was a brunette. She was short and slender and wore a tight, mauve cocktail dress with a pencil skirt and a halter neck that left her back bare. The swell of her breasts under the material was impressive considering the dress made it impossible for her to wear a bra. She had a narrow waist and snake-like hips which merged smoothly into her slender thighs. Her feet were small and clad in black suede high heels. 'You must be Amanda. I'm Natasha.'

She beckoned Amanda in then closed the door behind her and extended her hand. It was small and delicate. She wore a single gold wedding band and no other jewellery. Amanda shook it with a thin smile.

Amanda followed her into the sitting room. The house was large and grand, the ceilings high and worked in elaborate plaster cornicing.

'What can I get you to drink? We're having champagne.'

'That would be lovely,' Amanda said, studying Natasha intently. She was a beautiful woman. Her face was very symmetrical with a small mouth and small, but bright, light brown eyes. She wore a pancake make-up, like a model, so her complexion appeared flawless and her eyelashes were heavy with mascara. Her lips too had been painted with a bright red lipstick that made them stand out against the background of uniform, slightly tan make-up on the rest of her face.

'Maggie didn't lie,' Natasha said. There was a silver wine cooler on a sofa table behind a vast, cream sofa that dominated the room. A bottle of champagne nestled in the ice. Natasha poured the wine into a tall, crystal flute and handed it to Amanda, picking up her own glass at the same time.

'About what?'

'She said you were very attractive. Cheers.'

'Cheers.'

'And that this was only your second time.' She arched an eyebrow as her eyes examined Amanda from top to bottom.

'Yes.'

'Does that make you nervous?' The voice came from the other side of the room. A tall, slender man walked across the cream coloured carpet and held out his hand. 'I'm Adrian,' he said, shaking Amanda's hand. 'I'm delighted to meet you.'

He was older than his wife, around forty Amanda guessed. He had a tanned, weather-beaten complexion and very light blue eyes, which were sunken beneath a deep brow. The lower part of his face had a heavy blue shadow where he shaved. His hair was brown and luxuriant. He was wearing a pair of white cotton trousers and a black linen shirt.

'To answer your question, no, actually I don't feel in the least bit nervous,' Amanda said trying to keep cool. Adrian Chrystal was undoubtedly a very handsome man.

'We thought we'd show you around first,' Natasha said. She wrapped her arms around her husband's waist and hugged him affectionately. She was at least a foot shorter than him.

'It's a beautiful house.'

'We've had certain alterations made, to suit our . . .'

'Proclivities,' his wife finished the sentence for him.

'Would you like to see them?'

'I'd love to.'

'You mustn't be shocked,' Adrian said.

This suited Amanda's mood. She did not want to waste time on polite small talk. She had come to this house for sex. The appearance of her prospective partners had banished any reservations she might have had, and as far as she was concerned, and certainly as far as her body was concerned, she was ready to get on with it.

'Why should I be shocked?' she said. 'I'm very broad minded.' As she said it she realised it might not be true.

'This way, then,' Natasha said.

They led her through the sitting room into a large dining

room, at the end of which were two doors. One was open and she could see the kitchen beyond. The other was firmly closed. Natasha opened it and Amanda saw a flight of stairs leading down to a cellar.

'Please . . .' Adrian said, gesturing for her to take the lead.

Amanda walked down the thickly carpeted stairs. At the bottom she found herself in a large, rectangular room. It was carpeted in a red carpet not that dissimilar from the colour of her dress. One end of the room had a rostrum, like a small stage stretched across it, at the front of which were two Doric columns. With the exception of the wall behind the stage, which was covered with deep red velvet curtains, all the other walls were lined with red felt and looked as though they were padded. The ceiling too was treated in the same way. The material tended to deaden sound.

'This is what we call The Room,' Natasha said.

The room was far from empty. To the right was a large, walnut cupboard and a matching chest of drawers. In the middle was a big rectangular table that looked as though its legs had been shortened so it was at knee height. The surface of the table was covered with padded suede. To the side of this was a strange looking chair, made from tubular steel, with all sorts of knobs and slots obviously intended to alter its shape and purpose. There were two stirrups sticking up from its base, exactly like the type used in gynaecological examinations. Heavy black leather straps hung from various parts of the chair.

'Aldous Huxley,' Adrian said, tapping the chair with his hand. 'The gates of heaven and the doors of hell,' he said.

'My favourite,' his wife said pointedly.

The room was lit by a series of spotlights arranged on two bars running parallel along either side of the ceiling. Suspended between these were a number of bars and what were undoubtedly manacles, either leather ones or medieval looking metal clamps. All hung from chains that disappeared through metal lined holes. It didn't take any imagination to guess what they were for.

Adrian operated a switch on a panel by the stage. The velvet curtains at the back swished open to reveal a stone wall that gave the impression of an old dungeon. Attached to it, at various heights, were metal rings, from which hung more cuffs, most of these of the leather variety, though there was also a number of modern looking metal handcuffs, their shiny chrome glinting in the light. A rack on the same wall held an assortment of whips and paddles. Sticking out from the front of the stage was a cantilevered board, with a rounded outer edge a bit like a diving board. Leather straps hung from its middle section and there were leather cuffs attached to the stage end.

'We modelled this on *The Story of O*,' Natasha said, picking up the thick leather strap on the board, then letting it drop.

'As you see, we firmly believe that variety is the spice of life,' Adrian added.

Amanda remembered Maggie telling her some time ago about a man she had met who had been into what she had described as S & M. He had asked her to chain him to a special frame and tease him mercilessly. She had obliged and, she'd said, enjoyed every minute. Amanda couldn't help wondering if the story had been an edited version of what had gone on here with the Chrystals.

She was having trouble sorting out her reaction. There was a part of her that wanted to run. She had stumbled into something much more complex than she'd been given to understand and she wasn't at all sure that it didn't scare her. There was another side of her, however, that was profoundly interested, and was trying to imagine what exactly went on in this room, and what it would feel like to be bound and helpless in one of the many ways that were available here.

Natasha went to the large, walnut cupboard and opened the doors. Amanda smelt the unmistakable aroma of rubber. One half of the cupboard was occupied by clothes hanging from a rail. There were dresses in red, black and white in various styles, most of them with short skirts. There were

70

also garments made from vinyl and leather: skirts, trousers, blouses and pants. The other half of the cupboard was divided into shelving. Stacked here were high heeled shoes, wigs, and tangles of leather harnesses.

'We can cater to every taste,' Adrian said.

'But we have a rule.' Natasha closed the cupboard door.

'A very strict rule.'

'If we become friends,' Natasha said.

'If we like each other, and please each other,' Adrian added.

'Then we can experiment down here.'

'But never . . .'

'Never . . .'

'On the first . . . how shall we put it? Never on the first date.'

Amanda wasn't sure whether she was disappointed or relieved at this information.

'Has Maggie been down here with you?' she asked.

Natasha laughed. 'Of course. Didn't she tell you?'

'Maggie can be very imaginative,' Adrian said.

They led her back upstairs. In the sitting room Adrian poured more champagne.

'Is that what you're into, S&M?' Amanda asked, taking a large gulp of the wine.

'Yes and no. We are into everything. We like to experiment, as I said. We like to find what most pleases our friends and in the process we often find new diversions for ourselves. We are fortunately very well off so we can indulge our every whim,' Adrian explained.

'Don't you have any preferences?'

'How do you mean?' Natasha asked.

'Well, I mean, who gets tied up for instance?'

Adrian laughed. 'It doesn't really work like that. In our experience sadism and masochism are the same impulse, the same need. In fact, if we plan to go down to the room we toss a coin. The winner gets to decide what role they want to play.'

'What role?' Amanda asked.

'There are so many ways to describe it. Bottom and top. Slave and master. Masochist and sadist. We both get pleasure from being both. And with our friends along to assist . . . well, it is remarkably civilised.'

'We think it's only right to show you at the beginning, so you know what we're like. If you come back, if you want to come back, then we hope you'll want to go to the room with us,' Natasha said.

'And that's why we never indulge in all that on the first night. You have to work it out for yourself. Do you understand?'

'I think so.'

'Which brings us to tonight,' Adrian said. 'Unless, of course, you think we're perverted beyond belief and want to run out screaming into the night.'

Amanda knew the answer to that. Any misgivings she had experienced down in the cellar had been conquered by what she could only describe as lust. She desperately wanted to feel Adrian's body against hers. She wanted to kiss and suck his cock. She wanted it inside her. She wanted Natasha too. She had an almost overwhelming desire to lift that tight skirt and kiss her labia. She wanted to dig her fingers into those firm breasts and feel her tongue sinking into that small, painted mouth. The wonderful and so recently discovered thing was that she could do it all.

'I think that's the last thing I want to do,' she said calmly, looking from Natasha to Adrian with a steady gaze.

'You're wearing a basque,' Natasha said. 'Very sexy, don't you think, Ade?' She put her arms around her husband's waist again.

'I can see the suspenders,' he said.

'There's something about stockings, isn't there?'

'What do you want me to do?' Amanda said.

'So very willing,' Adrian commented. 'Since you come in such a delightful outfit why don't you show it to us?'

72

'All right.'

Amanda's heart was pounding. Everything was so casual, so matter-of-fact, as if they were asking her to show them a new dress. She remembered Annie saying how reluctance was born of the sexual taboos implicit in society. That was perfectly true, she had thought, and she was quite determined to show she had become taboo-free.

She wriggled the hem of the jersey dress up over her thighs, revealing the taut black stocking tops. She bunched it around her waist then pulled it up over her head and threw it on to the sofa. She stood in front of them, two perfect strangers, and watched as their eyes stared at her tightly corseted body while she combed out her short hair with her fingers.

'I think it's our turn, darling,' Natasha said.

'Quite lovely,' Adrian murmured, heading for the hall door. 'I'll only be a couple of minutes,' he added.

Amanda heard his footsteps going upstairs.

'Which do you prefer?' Natasha asked.

'Prefer?'

'Men or women?'

'I like both. This is all very new to me.'

'That's good, isn't it?'

'I'd like to know what to do,' Amanda said.

'What you're doing is just fine.'

'Good.'

Amanda took two steps forward and wrapped her arms around Natasha's waist, pulling her body into an embrace as she kissed her hard on the lips, forcing her tongue into her mouth. She felt her body shudder as Natasha's softness seemed to melt into her. Boldly, without thinking what she was doing, she pushed her hand into the cleft of Natasha's buttocks, pressing the skirt into her sex.

'You certainly know what you want,' Natasha said.

'Apparently I do,' Amanda agreed, surprised at her own forthrightness.

'Unzip me, then.'

Natasha turned and Amanda saw the collar of the halter neck had a short zip at the nape of her neck. She undid it and the front of the dress fell free. Natasha turned, revealing her very round, very high breasts. Her nipples were a deep brown colour, but were very small, no bigger than a cranberry. Her skin was whiter than the make-up she used on her face.

She wriggled the dress down over her hips. She was wearing tights but their gusset had been removed, exposing the whole area of her pubis, her sex and the cleft of her buttocks. Her pubic hair was black and curly but it had been very severely trimmed, the hair on her mons shaped like a cigar, with much of her labia entirely shaved.

'I've never seen those before,' Amanda said.

'Ade loves stockings but these drive him wild too. Come on. Let's go up.'

She took Amanda's hand and led the way into the hall and up a wide, straight staircase.

'Another special room?' Amanda asked.

'No, just our bedroom,' Natasha said. 'Though we do have a big bed.'

She opened a door at the end of the first floor landing. The lights in the room beyond were so dim that when she closed the door behind them it took Amanda a moment to adjust. There was a big, low double bed. The bedding had been stripped away, the mattress covered with a single white linen sheet.

Adrian lay on his back in the middle of the bed. He was naked. He held his cock in his fist. It was big, the glans protruding above his fingers.

'Well, look at you,' he said, wanking his erection slowly.

He was slender and well muscled. Unlike his wife, his body was as deeply tanned as his face apart from whiteness around his hips where he had clearly worn very brief trunks in the sun. Apart from a few stray hairs around his nipples, and a thick thatch of pubic hair, his chest and legs were hairless.

'There're so many possibilities, aren't there?' he said.

Natasha knelt on the bed. She leant forward and kissed the head of her husband's cock. He pulled his hand away to allow her to slowly swallow the rest of it. At the same time Natasha wriggled her knees apart, positioning herself so the whole slit of her sex was pointing directly at Amanda. It too had been carefully trimmed and depilated, so what was obviously a very prolific growth of black hair was not allowed to obscure her labia and the puckered corona of her anus. Her labia were thin and delicate.

Amanda stared at the spectacle for a moment. The black nylon tights framed the picture perfectly, Natasha's labia glistening and wet, the mouth of her vagina open. She felt an extraordinary thrill of excitement, as though her clitoris had been plucked like the string of a harp.

'You know what she wants, don't you?' Adrian said, looking straight into Amanda's eyes.

'Mmmm . . .' Natasha murmured, wriggling her bottom from side to side.

It was what Amanda wanted too. She drew the red panties down over her stockings, enjoying the way Adrian followed the garment all the way down to her ankles. As she stepped out of them she saw his eyes go back to the delta of her mons, staring at it intently. Then she climbed up onto the bed behind Natasha and caressed her small, rather sharp, buttocks. She lowered her head and inhaled the musky aroma of sex. Sticking out her tongue she wriggled it against Natasha's anus, then licked the length of her labia, using the whole breadth to part the folds of flesh, licking it like an ice cream cone.

Natasha said something but the word was gagged on her husband's cock. It sounded like, 'Higher.'

Amanda's hands caressed her hips as her tongue searched for the nut of her clitoris. It was not difficult to find. As the tip of her tongue pressed against it, Natasha grunted loudly, her body shuddering.

She could see Adrian's eyes looking at her, drinking in the details of her body, the way the tight basque moulded it and the suspenders held the stockings, taut at the side and back, and looping down loosely at the front. It was exciting. But then everything was exciting. Somewhere in the back of her mind she thanked her lucky stars that Maggie had got her into all this.

Natasha pulled off her husband's cock. She rolled over onto her back and wriggled so that she was positioned beneath Amanda's body until her head was under Amanda's belly. Almost before Amanda realised what Natasha was doing, she had hooked her arms around her back and raised her head, so her mouth buried itself in Amanda's labia, at the same time spreading her thighs apart to present Amanda with her own sex once again.

Amanda did not hesitate. As Natasha's tongue probed between her nether lips and found her already engorged clit, she dipped her head down to the brunette's sex and did exactly the same thing. The impact on her was extraordinary. A circle had been completed, their bodies were joined. Everything Amanda felt, the waves of pleasure emanating from her clit, she could feel in Natasha, the sensations doubled. More than doubled. There was another tier of pleasure too, the memory of how Monica had first done this to her and taught her, in turn, how to return the compliment.

Out of the corner of her eye she saw Adrian crawling around behind her. She knew what he was going to do. He positioned himself so he was crouched over her and slid his cock down between her buttocks to where his wife's mouth lapped at her sex. It was radiating heat.

She tried to concentrate on Natasha. Like hers, the woman's body was trembling with arousal, the first tendrils of orgasm were already beginning to wrap around her, inexorably tightening their grip. She could feel Natasha's pleasure as acutely as she could feel her own. She circled her tongue around the little promontory, each circuit taking exactly the same length of time as those Natasha was making on her.

Suddenly, the circle was broken. Natasha dropped her head

back onto the bed, but as Amanda was about to protest she felt Adrian's cock being pulled down to the mouth of her vagina by his wife's hand. He lunged forward and she felt his hard, incredibly hot phallus lance into her, her silky and soaking wet cunt parting to admit it. In one stroke he had filled her completely. His cock was big. His glans nosed against the neck of her womb, the base of his cock wide enough to stretch her labia around it deliciously.

Amanda felt her sex clench, contracting around the invader as if to test its strength. It was hard. Like steel. A steel rod pistoning in and out of her. Amanda moaned. She was coming now, rapidly. She tried to keep her tongue hard against Natasha's clit as she knew the brunette was coming too.

Adrian ploughed into her. Each stroke was an exercise in ecstasy. She had the softness of a woman on her mouth and the hardness of a man in her cunt. She had it all. Her body and her mind were perfectly in tune, the physical sensations in one increased by the flow of pure exhilaration in the other.

Her orgasm crashed over her. Somewhere in the maelstrom of feeling she knew Natasha was coming too. Their bodies shuddered, mashed together.

As she came out of it, as the flames of passion gradually died down, the first thing she was aware of was Adrian's cock jerking wildly inside her. At first Amanda thought he was spunking but then she realised his reaction had been caused by something else. Natasha had raised her head and gathered his balls in to her mouth one by one and was now sucking on them gently.

His cock sunk into Amanda's sex once more, but this time he did not withdraw. He did nothing. He didn't have to do anything. Natasha was doing it all for him, making his balls churn, his spunk rise.

Amanda wanted to be part of it too. She contracted her sex around him as hard as she could. The muscles in her sex were strong and she gripped the big rod as tightly as if it were in her fist. She held every inch of him. He was pulsing, his spunk ready to boil out. But she would not allow it. She held him back, squeezing his cock so hard his juices were trapped.

He wriggled, his wife's mouth making his need worse, her tongue licking his balls now, moving from one to the other.

'Please,' he said desperately.

Amanda worked her hands under Natasha's buttocks, lifting them off the bed. Then she dropped her lips back onto Natasha's sex, sucking on her labia and forcing her tongue up into her vagina. The effect was to produce a moan of pleasure from the other woman, the exhalation of hot air confined in her mouth so it played over her husband's balls, provoking him even further.

'Please,' he repeated.

With her tongue, Amanda licked the mouth of Natasha's vagina, lapping at her juices. They tasted wonderful. She remembered how Monica had tasted and how that taste had lingered with her for so long. Now it was back.

She tightened her grip, clenching the muscles of her cunt even more strongly. Adrian made an odd sound halfway between a moan and a cough. But the contraction not only affected him, it created a wave of feeling in Amanda too, a wave that suddenly pitched her toward a second orgasm.

Three things happened almost simultaneously. Amanda squirmed her fingers under Natasha's nylon-sheathed thighs and pushed two, then three, deep into her vagina, just as Natasha allowed her husband's balls to slip from her lips and transferred her attention to the little nub of Amanda's clitoris, exposed by the fact her labia were stretched apart by the breadth of the cock buried between them. The double impact of feeling Natasha's silky wet vagina clinging to her fingers, and her tongue artfully playing her clit like a tiny stringed instrument, produced the third event. An orgasm blossomed in her sex, streaking out from her clit, up the whole length of her body, into every nerve and sinew. Her eyes rolled back, a sharp almost painful pleasure concentrated behind her eyeballs and she went rigid, her sex gripping even tighter than it had been before.

It lasted forever. Or almost.

But then, as it melted away, her body melted too. Adrian felt her sex turn to jelly, a flood of juices washing over it. Instantly his cock spasmed, free at last. Spunk shot out of him. It spattered against the yielding flesh, jet after jet of it. It was so hot he was sure he could feel it as it started to run down inside her.

He rolled onto his back and watched as the two women sat up.

'Kiss me,' Amanda said. She pulled the brunette closer and licked her mouth, wanting to taste her own juices. She could feel Natasha's breasts too, crushed into her own. Despite the basque she could feel her tiny nipples as hard as stone.

But Natasha had her own ideas in that department. Without breaking the kiss she pushed Amanda back on to the bed until she was lying flat. Then she moved her mouth down to Amanda's throat, sucking and licking and tonguing the flesh as her hand came up and folded the bra cups of the basque down, tucking them neatly under her breasts one by one. With the nipples exposed she worked her mouth down and sucked them hard, each in turn, her teeth pinching them then allowing her tongue to push the little buds back into the spongy mass. Amanda moaned, her breasts tingling. Men had done this to her so many times. Why was it so different with a woman?

Amanda spread her thighs apart eagerly. After the intensity of her last orgasm moments before she wouldn't have believed herself capable of wanting more, but her body clearly felt differently. Natasha took the hint, moving her mouth down Amanda's belly. As Natasha's tongue parted her labia again she felt her clitoris tense, eager, it seemed, as ever.

Her clit reacted to the first touch with a spasm of pleasure. She moaned loudly.

But that was not Natasha's goal. She moved lower and

pushed her tongue into the mouth of Amanda's vagina. She wanted her husband's spunk. Like a strange cocktail it was mixed with the taste of Amanda's sex. Enthusiastically she lapped it up. Then, when her tongue had reached as far up as it could go, she brought her hand around Amanda's thigh, the jet black welt of the stocking stretched out by the suspender, and dipped her fingers into her vagina too, like a bear's paw in the honey pot, drawing out more of the precious fluid, her mouth sucking it off eagerly.

Amanda's body was trembling. This treatment was producing new shards of pleasure. Again an orgasm was threatening, the clouds of feeling gathering, with nothing she could do, or wanted to do for that matter, to prevent it.

Adrian got to his knees. He crawled up to Amanda and leant forward so his flaccid cock was rising against her cheek. Turning her head to the side Amanda gobbled it up, able to take his cock and his balls into her mouth, just as Natasha decided the honey pot was empty and transferred her attention back to Amanda's clit.

Natasha was kneeling to one side of Amanda's body, her husband to the other. Amanda could not see the brunette but groped around with her hand until she touched her bottom. She worked her way up the tight nylon until it gave way to flesh. Parting the lips of her sex with her fingers, she plunged two inside Natasha's cunt, screwing them around until they were as deep as they would go, her knuckles grinding against the woman's thin labia.

Then they were all joined, a circle of three, the point of connection between each producing exquisite pleasure. Adrian's cock was growing rapidly as Amanda stroked his glans with her tongue. One of his balls slipped out of her mouth. Soon he was so big she could not contain the other one either.

Natasha's tongue was relentless. She had left her fingers in Amanda's vagina and now slid another to the puckered crown of her anus. The juices from her sex had lubricated the little hole and there was no resistance as Natasha's finger slid inside and Amanda gasped with pleasure. She recovered quickly and worked her own fingers down in exactly the same way.

Amanda was coming again, harder and faster than she had come before. Instinctively she moved her mouth back and forth on Adrian's cock, as her fingers pistoned into Natasha's body with the same rhythm. Again, she could feel Natasha's pleasure as vividly as she could feel her own, her mouth and her sex perfect conduits for her sexual emotions. But this time she could feel Adrian too, his cock pulsing every time she forced it deep into the back of her throat.

Natasha was wriggling her buttocks from side to side as if trying to screw Amanda's finger further into her sex. Amanda thought the brunette was coming, but as the woman's mouth seemed to melt over her sex, as if merging with it, her own climax exploded. Her mouth opened as if to scream, the sensation of pleasure so extreme, but any sound was gagged on the flesh that used the opportunity to push deeper into her throat, pulsing wildly and producing, amazingly, another ejaculation.

Chapter Five

The house was dark, with no lights showing. That either meant that Greg had already gone to bed, or that he wasn't home yet.

Amanda paid off the black cab she had hailed in Kensington and walked up to her front door. She felt distinctly light-headed and not quite in touch with the real world. Her sex was sore and sensitive after the hammering it had taken and her labia were swollen, so swollen she could feel them rubbing together as she walked. Or was that just a product of her vivid imagination? She let herself into the house. Greg's car keys were not on the little hook by the front door, so it meant he wasn't home yet, and Amanda breathed a sigh of relief. As he would certainly have started to ask questions if he'd seen her in the red basque and ankle boots – hardly the outfit for going to the cinema – she'd planned to change her lingerie and shoes in the downstairs cloakroom. She'd left plain cotton underwear in there and a pair of flat-heeled shoes hidden behind the bleach bottles under the sink. Now she didn't have to bother.

In the bedroom she pulled the jersey dress over her head and quickly unhooked the basque. It had left deep indentations in her flesh. She stripped off the stockings. Her discarded panties were still in her handbag and she stuffed them and the rest of the lingerie into the back of the wardrobe until they could be washed in the morning. She didn't want to risk Greg finding them in the wicker laundry basket with the rest of the dirty clothes. Especially her panties, which were very much the worse for wear, her excitement having left its mark.

She ran a shower and was just stepping out of the bathroom, with a towel in her hand, when she heard the key in the front door. His footsteps mounted the stairs.

'Hi,' she said, towelling her naked body dry.

'Bloody Max,' he said, trying to tear his tie off and in the process half strangling himself.

'What's he done now?' She rubbed the towel between her legs.

'Always calls me into his office just as I'm about to leave. Asked me to go to see Chambers.'

'At night?'

'Exactly. They're working on some new development.'

She towelled her breasts. Her nipples reacted with a little twinge of pleasure.

'What are these doing out?'

He was staring at the ankle boots. She had left them by the foot of the bed and forgotten to put them away.

'Oh . . .' Damn, she had to try and think of something quickly. 'I was trying them on again.'

'What for?'

'I was thinking about seducing you.'

He went into the bathroom, apparently satisfied with that explanation. Quickly Amanda shoved the boots back into the wardrobe.

She heard the shower running.

'How was the movie?' he shouted.

'Dreary,' she replied. She put on the white silk pyjama top she wore to bed and slid between the sheets, turning on her bedside light and picking up her book. She liked to read a few pages every night before she went to sleep.

The shower stopped. She heard him cleaning his teeth. The words on the page she was reading didn't register. With her legs together her clitoris was pressed between her labia. It was so hard it felt like a dried pea. The princess and the pea, she thought, smiling to herself. Perhaps that was the real significance of that fairy story.

'What's this?' he said, coming out of the bathroom. He was naked. His once strong and slender body had softened and he was developing an incipient paunch, a slight roundness to his belly which had once been flat.

'What's what?' she asked, putting down the book.

'I thought you were planning to seduce me.' He was looking around for the boots.

'I didn't think you'd be interested.' She couldn't believe that of all nights he would choose tonight to be interested in sex.

'I wasn't. But since you suggested it . . .'

'I didn't mean . . .'

'Oh, hold on, have you got a surprise for me?' He took the corner of the bedding and stripped it away, revealing her legs. 'Oh.' He was expecting her to be hiding stockings and suspenders or some other variation on a theme. He looked geniunely disappointed.

'I just thought . . .' she said, trying to think of something to say.

'Are you trying to wind me up?' he grumbled.

'I just thought,' she said quickly, getting out of bed, 'that you'd like to watch me.'

'Watch you?'

'A sort of reverse striptease. Does that appeal?'

'Mmmm . . . sounds good.' He sat on the bed, propping his head against the pillows. 'A nice little show.'

'Exactly.' She congratulated herself on her quick-thinking. The last thing in the world she wanted was more sex. But she clearly had no choice.

She opened the drawer of the chest where she kept all the lingerie, trying to remember the last time he'd shown any interest in her body. Perhaps the sexual glow which still enveloped her was giving off some sort of pheromones that were irresistible to the male, like a bitch on heat. On a cruder level, she was glad Natasha had done such an effective job of consuming her husband's copious ejaculation.

Amanda took out a wide black satin and lace suspender belt. Wrapping it around her waist she hooked it in place. Much to her surprise the feeling of constriction had an immediate effect on her. She felt a surge of arousal so strong she had to suppress a moan. A dozen images of what she had done, and what had been done to her, whirled through her mind. Apparently this was not going to be such a chore after all.

She pulled out a pair of black stockings. They were fully fashioned with a seam. Sitting in the small bedroom chair in one corner of the room she bunched the nylon and raised her leg, making sure she was positioned so that her husband would be able to see her naked sex. Would he notice it was puffy and swollen? Would he see evidence to suggest that a woman had so recently and comprehensively tongued and penetrated it? The thought produced another thrill.

'I'm very turned on,' she said as she pulled the second stocking up her leg, raising her foot high into the air so her sex was completely exposed. 'Can you see that?'

'Are you wet?'

'Of course I'm wet, I've been thinking about sex all evening.' That was not a lie she thought.

She stood up. Standing with her feet apart she unbuttoned the pyjama top and pulled it off her shoulders. She took hold of her nipples with her fingers pulling her breasts up by them, stretching the flesh. A huge rush of feeling coursed through her, making her shudder. She saw his cock twitch. It was beginning to grow.

She walked over to the wardrobe, turning her back on him. She took out a pair of black patent leather shoes, the heels so high they held her feet almost vertically. An ankle strap extended from the back of the heel and she stopped to buckle it, making sure her bottom faced Greg squarely.

'I thought you were going to wear the boots?' he said.

'Changed my mind.' As soon as she'd secured the second shoe she wriggled her legs apart and grasped her ankles, knowing this would give him a spectacular view of her sex.

Then she took one hand and reached back between her legs, spreading her fingers wide apart over her buttocks. Slowly she slid her hand down the cleft of her buttocks, until her middle finger nosed into her labia. The first touch produced a shock of sensation so sharp it almost made her lose her balance. She managed to control herself and let her finger slide up to her clit, this time making sure she was braced for the impact.

'I like to see that,' Greg said.

Looking through her legs she could see he was fully erect now and had grasped his cock in his hand. There was a time when watching her masturbate had been a regular part of their sexual routine.

She wriggled her finger against her clit. It was sore but the soreness was delicious. She realised with a shock that her body was so sensitised, so sexually aware, that she could have come easily, just like this. A few more light touches and she would be on the brink.

But she didn't want that. If Greg had decided to revive their sex life she wanted to take full advantage of the fact, despite the exigencies she'd already experienced earlier on.

She straightened up and turned round. The stocking on her left leg had wrinkled around the knee so she put her foot up on the bed, an inch from Greg's side, and worked the palms of both hands sensuously up her leg, smoothing the nylon out until it was perfectly taut. She re-adjusted the clip of the suspender to hold the stocking more tightly then looked straight into her husband's eyes. She stepped up on to the bed, standing astride his body, her head almost touching the ceiling. With tiny little steps, the spiky heels digging into the sheet, she tottered forward until she was standing over his head and he could stare up into her sex.

'Nice view?' she asked.

'Great,' he said, caressing her leather shoes with both hands.

She backed off a little, then couched down on her haunches,

settling herself so his erection was just nosing into the cleft of her bottom. She put her hands on his chest.

'Just like the old days,' she said.

'Great,' he repeated. He bucked his hips, trying to push his cock into her vagina, but instead it slid up between her buttocks.

'What do you want?'

'Please . . .' he said. She felt another rush of sensation, the word reminding her of Adrian and how he too had begged. She was sure she could feel a flood of juices running down onto her thighs.

'Is this what you're so desperate for?' she asked, not in the mood for more teasing, her own need now too great. She twisted her hand behind her back, caught hold of his cock, slotted it into the mouth of her vagina and sunk her body down until she was sitting firmly on her hips and he was impaled inside her. He groaned. His hands shot up to her breasts, groping them none too gently, and he grunted loudly. His cock pulsed inside her a couple of times rather weakly.

Amanda ground herself down on him but oddly felt no response. It was only then she realised he'd come. She felt his cock softening already, a feeling of wetness spreading through her loins.

'Sorry,' he said. 'I just couldn't stop myself.'

She raised herself on her haunches and his cock flopped out of her, wrinkled and wet.

'And what am I supposed to do?' she said angrily.

'It's been such a long time, Mandy.'

'And who's fault is that?'

'I know, I know,' he said. 'You know I've been so busy at work. Let's have another go tomorrow night. Come on, better get some sleep now. I've got an early start in the morning.'

'That's it is it?'

'I'll get home early. You can get all togged up again, can't you?'

Amanda didn't reply. She sat on the edge of the bed and unbuckled her shoes, then peeled off the stockings. She should have known it was too good to be true. In another mood she might have been tempted to sit on his face and demand he licked her and sucked her until she came.

But in a sense his behaviour was welcome. It justified what she had done and the lies she had told. It confirmed that she was absolutely right to go out and get a sex life for herself because he was certainly not going to make the slightest effort in that direction.

Leaving the lingerie on top of the chest of drawers, Amanda pulled on the pyjama top and got into bed, turning off the light. She lay feeling the little trills and pulses that still played in her body. A wetness was leaking from her sex. She thought about Adrian. She thought about Natasha. As they'd said goodbye to her at the door, Adrian said he hoped she'd come again. The way he'd put it made them all laugh. But Amanda wanted to return very much indeed, and what had just happened with Greg had made that need even more urgent.

'Hi.'

They kissed on both cheeks, like old friends. It was Sunday afternoon and Amanda was supposed to be going to the new exhibition at the Tate with Maggie.

As the woman's lips brushed hers, Amanda felt an instant rush of desire. Natasha was wearing cream silk lounging pants and a matching top, the material shiny, soft and voluminous. Once again her face was heavily made-up, the pancake foundation slightly whiter this time, the extensive eye make-up, by contrast, even darker. Her eyelashes were so long, brushed into a curl with mascara, that Amanda wondered if they were false.

She closed the front door and led the way into the sitting room. A bottle of champagne was already open.

'Would you like a glass?'

'Thank you.'

She poured the wine and handed Amanda the crystal flute. They raised their glasses in a silent salutation.

'We were very glad you called again,' Natasha said.

'Didn't you think I would?'

'You were very . . . enthusiastic. Since it was only your second time we wondered if we might have gone too far.'

'Too far?'

'You know. Perhaps we should have taken it more slowly.'

'Don't be silly. Couldn't you see what a good time I was having? It was heavenly. Wonderful.'

'I'm glad.'

'I was hoping you wouldn't mind me calling again so soon.' It had only been five days since her last visit to the house.

'Of course not. I don't know who was more pleased, me or Adrian.'

'I wouldn't want to impose.' The fact was Amanda had had to restrain herself from calling on Wednesday. In the mood she was in at the moment she wished she could have spent every night at their house.

'So, where's Adrian?'

'Oh, he's a bit tied up at the moment. Sit down, let's finish the champagne and we'll go and find him.'

Amanda sat on the large sofa. She was wearing a grey suit and a black blouse and black suede high heels. To give her hosts what she hoped would be a pleasant surprise she was wearing nothing under the suit but a pair of gunmetal grey hold-up stockings.

'We didn't do much talking last time, did we?' Amanda said sipping her wine. It tasted good.

'No, it was all a bit sudden.'

'How did you get into all this?'

'Oh, Ade and I have always been very adventurous when it comes to sex. We actually met at an orgy.' She sat at the other end of the sofa, curling her legs up underneath her.

'An orgy?'

90

'Ugly word, isn't it? The French say *une partouse*. Sounds much more elegant and sophisticated doesn't it?'

'And that's where you met?' Amanda tried to hide her astonishment.

'I was going out with this very rich, but very kinky, man. He was into everything. When I say I was going out with him, I mean he had like a little harem, sometimes three, sometimes five or six women all living in the same house with him. He never had sex *à deux*.'

'Really?'

'But I knew what I was getting myself into. And I'd always liked women so in some ways it was the perfect arrangement. He bought us all beautiful clothes and jewellery and perfume and very expensive lingerie. All of us. And if one of the girls decided she couldn't take it any more she got to keep all the stuff. The longer you stayed the more you got. He bought three of us cars. I got a Jaguar. Jenny, she was his favourite, got a Ferrari. Mind you, he bought us a lot of other stuff. Like I said he was into everything. Rubber. Leather. S & M. He had these special rubber outfits made for us. Rubber panties and bras and rubber corsets. And dresses. Even rubber stockings and boots. Some of it looked quite good.

'Anyway, he used to hold some pretty wild parties. He'd invite a whole load of men, his business connections and associates I guess, and hire two or three girls for each of them. The girls had to get dressed up in all sorts of exotic stuff, thigh boots, cupless bras, leather harnesses. The guys just couldn't resist. There was champagne by the case-load and it would soon get pretty raunchy. And we were all there too, with Bob. That was his name, Bob Beamer. He'd have us all dressed up too, in whatever had taken his fancy, usually rubber. He had built a circular rostrum in the middle of the room and he liked to do it up there so everyone could see. He liked to watch too. And though the guys didn't know it, he taped everything.'

'And that's where you met Adrian?'

'He was one of the guests. I was wearing this rubber catsuit with a full helmet. Everything covered in shiny black rubber except my eyes, my mouth, my tits, and my fanny. He told me he was turned on by the idea of fucking someone he wouldn't be able to recognise afterwards.'

'But he did?'

'No. I liked him so much I went after him. I got changed quick. Caught him as he got into his car.'

'And you left Bob?'

'Eventually. The thing was after that we both found it difficult to settle for conventional sex. Sometimes Bob had asked couples to his parties where he knew the wife was, shall we say, sexually liberated. Adrian had befriended one of them. We started seeing them.'

'Going to bed with them?'

'Yes.'

'And they introduced us to *Contacts*.'

'And that's how you met Maggie?'

'Yes. She replied to one of our ads.'

Amanda looked at Natasha and discovered the brunette was looking straight at her. Their eyes met and Amanda felt a hard pulse of lust. For some reason she suddenly had a very clear image of Maggie O'Keefe and Natasha locked in each other's arms. 'You're a very beautiful woman,' she said calmly.

'Thank you. You're lovely too. Adrian thought you were great.'

'He was amazing,' Amanda said and meant it.

'It's a little trick he's developed. He can hold back part of his ejaculation.'

'That's how he does it.' She had wondered. Even in her youth, when she'd been with virile young boys at the height of their sexual energy, she couldn't remember any who had been able to come twice in such a short space of time.

Natasha put down her champagne glass and stood up. 'Talking off which . . .'

She held out her hand to help Amanda up. Amanda took it

but as she got to her feet she wrapped her arms around Natasha and kissed her full on the mouth. As Natasha responded, her tongue dancing against Amanda's, their bodies writhed against each other, their pubic bones grinding together.

'Lovely,' Amanda breathed without breaking the kiss, their mouths hot and wet. She sent her hand between their bodies to find Natasha's left breast and squeezed it hard, through what was obviously her bra. She pinched her tiny nipple and felt Natasha's body squirm. Her other hand drove down between her buttocks. She was taller than the brunette but managed to get her hand right down between her legs, pushing the silky gusset of the lounging suit into her labia. Even through the material she could tell that Natasha's sex was already moist.

'Come on,' Natasha said, breaking away with obvious reluctance.

'Oh yes, that's the rule, isn't it?'

'The rule?' Natasha looked puzzled.

'Everything together.' Amanda was remembering what Annie had told her.

'No, we're not like that. I don't mind what Ade does when I'm not there. Obviously, it's the same for him. In fact, he rather likes the thought that I'm here with someone. If he's really lucky I video it all for him and we play it back later.'

Amanda felt her clitoris flex against her labia. That idea excited her. 'Have you done that with Maggie?' she asked almost before she realised what she'd said.

'Yes, as a matter of fact I have. Once. Do you want to see the tape?'

'No,' Amanda said, too quickly. The thought of seeing her friend in bed with another woman was a step too far for her. Since she'd discovered that Maggie shared the same sexual tastes as her she had been unable to stop herself wondering what it would be like to take their relationship one step further. She was afraid it would kill their friendship, however, and had deliberately tried not to think of Maggie as a sex object. It had proved difficult. Maggie's ample figure and lovely face had a way of stealing up on her. She certainly didn't want to stir up those feelings by seeing Maggie and Natasha together, doing things she had tried so hard not to imagine.

'Maggie wouldn't mind,' Natasha said, thinking that was the reason for Amanda's reluctance. 'In fact I'm sure she'd like the idea.'

'What makes you say that?'

'Oh, come on, you two are friends, right? Haven't you ever . . .'

'No,' Amanda said firmly.

'I must have got the wrong end of the stick. From what Maggie said I thought . . .'

'From what Maggie said?'

'Yes.'

'Like what?' Amanda's pulse was racing.

'Just she thought you were edible. And I agree with her. You are. Come on let's go and find Ade.'

She took Amanda's hand and led her into the hall.

Amanda would have liked to have questioned her more closely on what Maggie had said, but decided this was not the time or place. She stored the information away and perhaps would continue the discussion with Maggie herself.

'Where are we going?'

'The room.' Natasha said. 'Don't you remember? This is your second visit, after all.'

Oddly, Amanda had completely forgotten about the room. She had been so preoccupied by what had happened upstairs she hadn't dwelt on what they had shown her in the cellar. Now she felt a sudden *frisson* of fear as Natasha opened the cellar door. She remembered the whips and chains and all the other paraphernalia.

'I don't know . . . I'm not sure . . .' she said, resisting the pressure of Natasha's hand on her shoulder to move down the carpeted stairs. 'I've never done anything like this.'

'Don't worry,' Natasha said. 'If you don't like it you say no. We're not going to force you.'

Amanda looked at her. Her light brown eyes were reassuring. So far the risks she had taken had paid enormous dividends. This was not the moment to become faint-hearted. She smiled a thin smile, then started down the steps.

There were lights illuminating the staircase but they did not reach into the Stygian gloom of the rest of the large space. Natasha turned on a switch at the bottom of the stairs. A bank of spotlights came up, lighting the centre of the room.

'Come on,' Natasha said. She took Amanda's hand and led her forward.

Amanda was agog. A narrow, low bench had been placed in the centre of the room. It was about six feet long and no more than eighteen inches wide. Adrian was lying on it. At least Amanda assumed it was Adrian, she could not see his face. It was covered in a rubber helmet, so thin it fitted like a second skin, moulding itself to his features. The only gap in the material was a small hole which exposed his nostrils and a large oval through which she could see his mouth.

The rest of his body was swathed in rubber too. Strips of black rubber had been wrapped around it, rather like an Egyptian mummy, binding his arms to his sides and his legs tightly together. The rubber criss-crossed his chest and stomach, but had been arranged in such a way to leave his cock and balls exposed. His cock was erect, standing up vertically from his rubber-covered belly.

Five thick leather straps had been stretched over his body and around under the bench. There was one at his chest, waist, at the top of his thighs, and just above the knee and at the ankles. The net result was that he could not move his body an inch. Only his head was free to move, though the range of his neck muscles was very limited.

'Well,' Natasha asked, 'what do you think?'

'He likes this?' Amanda said, her voice croaking with astonishment.

'He doesn't have a choice. We told you, we toss a coin.

95

He lost. Actually he's lost for the last four occasions. I'm on a winning streak. Doesn't it make you hot?'

The simple answer to that was yes. Amanda had never seen anything like this before but the prostrate and helpless body and the huge cock that rose from it was undoubtedly turning her on. 'So, what do we do?' she asked.

'Anything we want. Here, let me help you.'

Natasha helped Amanda off with her jacket and went to hang it up. As calmly as she could, though calm was the last thing she felt, Amanda unzipped her skirt and stepped out of it, then stripped off her blouse, expecting a response.

She got it. 'Look at you! You should see her, Adrian. She's just taken off her suit and blouse and she's not wearing anything but a pair of hold-ups. Isn't she a naughty girl?'

Adrian's cock twitched. 'Let me see her,' he said pleadingly.

'Don't be silly,' Natasha replied. 'What makes you think you're going to be allowed any privileges?' Natasha winked at Amanda and smiled. She unbuttoned the top of the lounging suit and pulled it off. She was wearing a white satin bra. She shimmied out of the trousers, revealing panties in the same material. 'Unhook me,' she said to Amanda, turning her back to give her access to the clip of the bra.

Amanda released the double hooks. She pressed her naked breasts into Natasha's shoulders and ran her hands around and under her breasts, lifting the cups and sinking her fingers into the warm flesh, taking reassurance as well as pleasure from this more familiar contact. She kissed Natasha's neck, and inhaled her strong, musky perfume. Her whole body came alive, her misgivings vanished. This was going to be another new experience to add to the growing list.

She ran one hand down into the front of Natasha's satin panties, pushing down between her legs until her finger was lodged between her labia and she could feel her clitoris. It was throbbing. She pushed it to one side and then over to the other. Natasha moaned, arching her head back until it rested on Amanda's shoulder.

'Lovely,' she breathed, wriggling her buttocks from side to side, the soft flesh and satin rubbing against Amanda's naked belly. 'Does it excite you, seeing him like that?'

'Yes.' It was true. Adrian was bound and helpless. He was no longer a person, but an object. His wife had converted him into a living dildo, warm and animate but unable to express the slightest preference as to how he was to be used.

Amanda slid her finger deeper down the slit of Natasha's sex. She found the mouth of her vagina and twisted her finger into it. Natasha moaned.

'It obviously excites *you*,' she said. The brunette's sex was liquid.

Natasha broke away. She skimmed her panties down her slender legs and discarded the limp bra, her breasts trembling.

'So, what do I do?' Amanda asked.

'Whatever you want.'

Amanda knew exactly what she wanted. She'd known since she'd first seen that large, hard cock. Throwing aside the last of her inhibitions she simply straddled the bench, positioned her sex over the vertical phallus and dropped down on to it. The cock plunged into her, taking her breath away. 'Oh, God, that's good,' she muttered.

It was a bit like riding a horse. The height of the bench meant that her legs were bent at the knee, as they would be in stirrups, and the width of Adrian's body spread her thighs wide apart as a saddle would. She could lift herself off him with the greatest of ease, pushing up with her thigh muscles until his cock was almost entirely exposed. Alternatively she merely had to raise her feet from the floor for the weight of her body to sink down on him even more effectively, grinding her pubic bone against his and forcing his cock deeper.

Natasha came up behind her, her hands cupping both her breasts.

'Can you tell who it is?' she asked her husband.

Amanda felt his cock twitch inside her, one of the few movements he was capable of.

'Not you,' he said.

'Clever, isn't he?'

She dropped one of her hands to Amanda's belly, then moved her finger inward until it had found Amanda's clitoris. At the same time she kissed her neck and pinched her right nipple with the fingers of her other hand.

Amanda's body clenched. Slowly, almost unconsciously, she began to ride up and down on his phallus, raising herself no more than an inch, then dropping back on it and grinding her hips from side to side.

'He's so big,' she said.

'I'm going to make you come like this,' Natasha whispered into her ear. Her lips nibbled at the delicate whorls, then her tongue invaded them, pushing deep, making Amanda shudder. Natasha's finger stroked across her clit. She twisted her head around and kissed her full on the mouth.

An orgasm began to pluck at Amanda's nerves. The sensation of having a hard, hot cock buried in the depths of her while a soft, wet tongue explored her mouth and fingers pinched and played at her nipples and clit, was indescribable. She had never imagined such pleasure.

She could feel the heat of Adrian's body. Above the welts of her stockings the black rubber dragged against her flesh. She wondered if he would come. His cock was pulsing against the tight confines of her sex. As she thrust down on it his glans butted into the neck of the womb. She had the strange sensation that there was a little mouth there pursed to kiss the invader.

Her eyes closed. She wanted to keep them open to stare at Adrian's bound body, the sight of which thrilled her for reasons she did not properly understand. But she could not. The urgent feelings of her burgeoning orgasm were too strong. She needed no distractions. She needed darkness to concentrate on every wave of pleasure that washed over her, every erogenous zone on her body stimulated by Natasha and her husband.

She rose slightly then pushed down on him one last time. As Natasha's finger manipulated her clit and her other hand pinched sharply at her left nipple, the tension in Amanda's body snapped and she felt as if she were falling, plunging down into a pit of ecstasy.

She didn't feel Natasha moving away. The aftermath of orgasm, the gentle tremors and thrills of feeling that followed the explosion, lasted a long time and Amanda clung to them, wanting to cherish every last one, unwilling to open her eyes until they had vanished entirely.

When she did Natasha was facing her. She too had straddled the bench and was poised over her husband's mouth. Amanda could see his tongue licking between her thin labia.

'He's very good at this.' Natasha said, looking into Amanda's eyes.

'Shall we change places, then?' Amanda suggest boldly, her appetites far from satiated.

'What a good idea.'

Amanda climbed out of the saddle, or that's what it felt like to her. The withdrawal of Adrian's cock provoked a whole panoply of sensations that made her moan loudly but she controlled herself and watched as Natasha replaced her, taking the soaking wet and glistening phallus in her hand, then guiding it to the mouth of her vagina.

'He looks like he's going to burst, doesn't he?' Natasha said, nipping his cock between her fingers. 'Whose is it this time, darling?' she asked as she slowly sunk down on to his shaft. Amanda watched with fascination as the cock all but disappeared, stretching Natasha's thin labia around it.

'It's her again,' Adrian grunted.

'Wrong. Not so clever after all.' Natasha ground down on him, wriggling her hips from side to side. 'Come on, Mandy,' she said, nodding towards her husband's rubber-encased head.

Amanda did not need any encouragement. She swung her leg over the top end of the bench and bent her knees until her sex was brushing Adrian's mouth. It felt hot and wet. Immediately, his tongue probed her labia. Her orgasm had tenderised her nerves and she felt a sharp almost painful jab of sensation as the tip of his tongue found her enlarged clitoris. She groaned loudly, almost losing her balance, putting her hands out onto his black rubber covered chest to steady herself. Adrian's tongue did not withdraw, however. It tapped the swollen bud of nerves then licked it up and down with what was obviously well practised expertise.

'I love to see that,' Natasha said.

Amanda leant forward and kissed the brunette on the mouth lightly. Determined to give as good as she got she dug her fingers into the woman's right breast and pushed her other hand down between her legs. With her labia spread apart by Adrian's cock her clit was already exposed. Amanda moved her finger against it, feeling Natasha's whole body tremble in reaction.

'Yes . . .' she said, 'that's what I want.' And that's what she got. Amanda plucked at her clitoris like the strings of a harp as hers, in turn, was manipulated by Adrian's tongue. The three were joined again, as they had been on her last visit, each rush of feeling in one felt almost as acutely by the other two. It was a delicious circle. Adrian's insistent tongue provoked a wave of feeling in Amanda's body. Like electricity this travelled through Amanda's hands and into Natasha's clitoris and breast, making the brunette's body contract around the hard cock impaled inside it. That, in turn, produced a hard pulse of feeling in Adrian which Amanda could feel. And so it went on. They were all getting higher and hotter and near to the inevitable.

It was Natasha who toppled over the brink first. She grabbed Amanda's wrist, forcing her hand flat against her breast, the flesh ballooning around it, and wriggled herself down that last inch on her husband's cock. Her orgasm tore through her, making her whole body shudder.

The effect on Amanda was nearly as dramatic. The sight of

Natasha struggling with the intensity of feelings that rushed through her was one of the most erotic spectacles she had ever seen. She felt her own body readying itself for another onslaught, spurred on by what she was seeing, and Adrian's artful tongue worming up against her clit.

'No, not yet,' Natasha said as she recovered. 'We're not finished yet . . .'

With surprising energy, considering what she has just experienced, she pulled herself off her husband's erection.

'No!' he said in alarm. 'Not tonight, please,' he begged. He tried to buck his body upwards towards her but achieved not the smallest of thrusts.

'Oh yes,' Natasha said, swinging her leg off him and standing at his side.

She came up in front of Amanda and lifted her up, unplugging that connection too. As Amanda stepped back she took hold of the top of the rubber helmet and pulled it off Adrian's head. His face was revealed, covered in sweat and reddened by its constriction, his hair plastered back against his head, his eyes screwed up against the light.

'Now, back where you were, darling, but just lean forward, don't bend your knees.' Natasha positioned her so that she was straddling Adrian's head again, applying gentle pressure to her back to get her to bend forward and rest her hands on Adrian's hips.

Amanda's body was still needy. Despite the shattering orgasm, or maybe because of it, her desire to come again was urgent, more urgent than she thought she'd ever felt before. She looked down between her legs. Adrian's sweat-wreathed face was staring up into her sex, his eyes rooted to it. In this position her mouth was only inches from his cock and she could see it was strained to the limit, every vein prominent, the glans swollen and red.

Amanda heard Natasha move away for a moment and then she was back. She could feel something cold and hard touching her buttocks. Though she could not see it she knew immediately what it was: a dildo. The head of the hard plastic shell prodded against the mouth of her vagina, but at the same time to her surprise she felt a similiar sensation at the ring of her anus.

'Clever, isn't it?' Natasha said. In fact the dildo was shaped like an extended thumb and forefinger, one cylinder long, the other stubbly, though both were the same width.

Natasha pushed the twin phalluses slowly into Amanda's body, watching her husband's eyes staring at the spectacle. His whole body was rigid, his spunk poised against the very last barrier of control.

'Pretty, isn't it?' she said, taunting him.

'Please,' he begged.

Amanda had heard that tone before. Adrian was totally powerless and that thrilled her. As the two prongs forced their way deep into her body, Natasha's other hand slipped under her belly to her clit.

'You're going to come again,' she said, as her finger found the swollen clit and ironed it back against the underlining bone before jiggling it from side to side. It was not a question but a statement of fact.

'Oh yes, oh yes . . .' It was perfect. So perfect. Amanda looked down at Adrian's cock. A tear of fluid had formed at the slit. Natasha pulled the double dildo from Amanda's body, then began sawing it back and forth as her finger worked on her clit.

It was too much, too good. A huge crescendo of sound and fury gathered in Amanda's body, everything she saw and felt provoking her. As it reached its peak she forced herself back on the two heads of the dildo, feeling them pushing that extra inch into both passages of her body. Exactly at that moment she saw Adrian's cock contract, and a jet of white spunk arced up into her face. The hot spunk seemed to drive her orgasm higher and deeper, her eyes forced closed by the impact. It went on and on forever.

When she opened her eyes again it was a bit like waking

from a deep and dreamless sleep. For a moment she had a job remembering where she was. She looked down at the rubber figure underneath her. The black rubber was spattered with white gobs of spunk.

Gently Natasha eased the dildo out. Amanda shuddered.

'My turn again now, I think,' Natasha said, helping Amanda to move off the bench and straighten up.

And, of course, it was.

Chapter Six

'Amanda?'

Amanda had answered the phone in the kitchen. She recognised Natasha's voice immediately. She had explained that they should not call her in the evenings but that any time during offices hours on a weekday was all right.

'Hello, it's nice to hear your voice.'

'We've got a surprise for you. Are you free Thursday night?'

'Could be.'

'Great. Be here at seven. How are you feeling, by the way?'

'A bit dazed.'

'Me too. It was great, wasn't it? You're very special. Adrian's just crazy about you.'

'He actually enjoyed that?'

'I thought you could see that for yourself.'

'I thought it was pure frustration.'

'Haven't you ever imagined being tied up like that? I mean, your whole body completely powerless. Everything gets focused on your sex. If I lose the toss Adrian spreads me out on that plank. You remember, like in *The Story of O*, with my legs chained up and spread apart and my arms tied above my head. It's a fantastic turn on. Especially if I'm blindfolded and gagged. Perhaps we'll try that on you.'

'Is that the surprise?' Amanda wasn't sure how she felt about the idea.

'No, no. Something else.'

'I'll be there.'

'Great. Give me a call if you feel lonely meantime. Remember we haven't got any rules. You might even like seeing yourself on videotape.' Natasha laughed as she said it.

'I'll think about it.'

'Otherwise, see you on Thursday.'

They exchanged goodbyes.

It had been two days since her adventure in Kensington and what she said to Natasha had been entirely true. She was still dazed. In fact she had a job concentrating on anything she was doing, her mind drifting back to the bizarre room and its equally bizarrely clad occupant.

She'd expected Natasha to call. After Adrian had finally been released from his bondage they had gone upstairs and finished off another bottle of champagne. They asked her, solicitously, if she was all right, fearing that, on reflection, she might regret what she'd got involved in.

But she didn't. When they suggested she return for another session in the room she jumped at the idea.

She had no regrets. Her labia and anus were sore, her nipples slightly bruised and her clitoris apparently permanently swollen, but they were the scars of battle and she bore them proudly. A few weeks ago if Maggie had described to her what had happened in the cellar she would have dismissed it as kinky and perverted. In fact it had seemed a perfectly natural extension to the sexual games they were already playing. More than that, it had been terribly exciting. She still shuddered every time she thought of Adrian's spunk lashing up over her face as her own climax had peaked. Two into three won't go, but one and two together seemed to be the perfect equation.

She finished washing up the breakfast dishes and went back up to the bedroom. Yesterday afternoon in a newsagent's she never normally frequented, she found, high on the top shelf, the latest edition of *Contacts*. Like a guilty schoolgirl she'd hurried home with it and hid it in the one place she was sure

Greg would never find it. The drawer where the exotic lingerie was kept.

She hadn't had time to look at it then. Greg had come home early. She'd had to wait till now.

She lay on the unmade bed and began flicking through the pages. It was not, she told herself, that she was looking for another adventure. It was just out of interest or, more accurately, fascination.

A picture caught her eye. A slender woman in a plain skirt and blouse, with bare legs, ankle strap high heels and neat, bob-cut brown hair and glasses. The ad under the photograph read:

Convincing tv. attractive, slim and very sub seeks a woman who is into tvs. Will satisfy your every whim. Genuine photograph. Very sincere. Please call 43 42 67.

Amanda stared intently at the photograph. Apart from a slight boniness around the knees there was nothing to suggest that the woman in the photograph was in reality a man. What would that be like she wondered? She imagined the man standing in her bedroom doorway, waiting to be ordered around. Would he want to fuck her in pretty feminine lingerie and his wig?

There were two or three pages of single men, two Negros, an Asian man and a striking looking Adonis, with weightlifter's muscles, his obviously semi-flaccid cock a very creditable size. She read the latter's advertisement:

I am thirty and in shape. Come and let me show you the real thing. Couples welcome and party invites accepted. Guaranteed nine inches available for your pleasure. No fees. 20 96 80.

That made Amanda think of Adrian. She had never measured a man's penis in an erect condition and had no idea whether nine inches was large or not, though the man in the ad obviously thought it was something to boast about. She knew that Adrian was large, though, and she had certainly never felt a man buried so deep in her as when she'd straddled him on the bench.

She remembered what Natasha had said on the phone about the strange arrangement jutting from the rostrum in the room. How would it feel to be bound to that, as helplessly as Adrian had been bound, her legs splayed apart, her sex open and available to whatever attentions her tormentors deemed fit? She shuddered, but whether from fear or excitement she could not tell.

Another photograph caught her eye. Unlike most of the photographs of couples, this one had not been cropped to make one picture out of two, but was of a couple who stood close together, though not actually touching. The man was fully dressed in a suit and tie, which looked extremely odd among the naked and semi-naked men who filled the other pages. But despite his modesty there was something indefinably attractive about him. Perhaps it was the expression on his face – for once in full view – a look that suggested amusement at finding himself in this photograph and interest as to the outcome. His wife had a mass of auburn hair arranged in thick, soft curls down to her shoulders, with a fringe that covered most of her forehead. She was dressed in a white, heavily boned basque, white stockings pulled into peaks on her thighs by taut suspenders, and white, rather full-cut bikini panties and white high heels. She had a small bosom and a neat, trim figure and long, slender legs. Unlike her husband her face was turned away from the camera so it was partially hidden.

But there was something odd about the way the couple stood side by side and yet apart, that Amanda found fascinating. She read the ad below:

Educated couple seek women for hetero activities. Non-smokers essential. We will travel or accommodate. First

Most of the ads from couples she had read mentioned that the wife was AC/DC. It was odd, Amanda thought, that this ad specified the opposite. Presumably the wife was content to watch while her husband made love to the new recruit. It was a pity too, because she found she was very attracted to the woman in the white basque. There was just something about her, some indefinable quality, that shone out of the photograph. She realised it might be precisely the fact that she had stated so uneqivocally that she was straight that created the attraction. Perhaps Amanda might be able to change her mind?

She was wearing the track suit she normally wore around the house and functional cotton bra and knickers. Reading through the ads had created a sticky feeling between her legs and little twinges of pleasure, mixed with needles of pain in her overused sex.

She pressed her thighs together, imagining the couple standing by the side of the bed looking down at her. Her clitoris responded to the pressure with a pang of pleasure.

The idea of masturbating seemed faintly ridiculous after so much sex but she could feel her nipples puckering, pushing against the confines of her bra as if trying to pierce it. She rubbed her palm against her left nipple as gently as she could but it reacted with stinging pleasure that made her moan.

'No,' she said aloud. The couple stared back at her. The man's eyes seemed to be looking straight at her. Amanda moved her hand to her lap and slid her legs apart. The eyes followed her. Tentatively she brushed her hand against the gusset of the tracksuit. An enormous wave of feeling rushed over her.

She closed her eyes. Her mind filled with images, snap-shots of Natasha's naked body, her legs spread apart, of Adrian's bound body, like a cylinder of black rubber, of Annie and Phil, and the ads in the magazine. She started thinking about what Natasha had said on the phone, this time about the video. What would it be like to make love with her then see it all played back? She imagined the flickering screen and saw two women cavorting on the bed, one of them Natasha. But the other woman was not herself but Maggie . . .

'No,' she said firmly.

The phone saved her from herself. For the second time that morning it rang. She reached over to the bedside table not knowing whether she was relieved or annoyed.

'Mandy?'

'Maggie, how are you?' She hoped her voice didn't give away what she had just been thinking.

'Great. How about you? I was going to ask you around but I've got a conference in Manchester for the next couple of days. So as I was quiet I thought I'd give you a call instead.'

'Good 'cause I needed to talk to you. Are you doing anything on Thursday night?'

'Don't think I'll be back, why?'

'Damn. I wanted you to cover for me with Greg. I'd thought of saying you'd got tickets for the ballet. He hates the ballet.'

'Well I can do that anyway. He's hardly going to call me on Saturday morning, is he? And I'll be back by Sunday. We can meet over the garden fence and I'll throw in lots of references to *pliés* and *par-de-deux*.'

'Thanks.'

'Where are you going?'

'Guess.'

'Oh, really! I knew you'd like them. So you're having fun are you?'

'I'm not sure what I'm having, Maggie, but it's great. I feel alive again.'

'That good, eh?'

'Oh, yes. It's funny. I always used to love sex. But I can't remember it being this good. Perhaps my body's making

110

up for lost time, all those years I let Greg set the sexual agenda.'

'Perhaps. Well I'm glad you're having such a good time.'

'What about you? Any new conquests?'

'No. It's been very boring. I'm going to have to get the latest edition of *Contacts*. I haven't seen a bedable man for days.'

'There's sure to be some talent in Manchester.'

'Manchester?'

'You said you were going to Manchester,' Amanda reminded her.

'Oh right. I forgot. Yes, maybe I'll get lucky. Listen I'd better get on. Just as long as you're still having a good time.'

'I'm fine, Maggie. Thanks for calling.'

'See you soon.'

The taxi dropped her outside the door. She was wearing a black cocktail dress with a box collar, hemmed in diamanté. The dress was knee length but had a split at the side that gave glimpses of her thigh. She had never dared wear it with stockings before but tonight she had done just that.

Again Amanda felt her heart beating faster as she walked up the path to the Chrystals' front door. The excitement had started the moment she had got in the taxi but now it was reaching a peak, her breath short and her mouth dry. She did not know exactly what awaited her behind the panelled door but the idea of a surprise added an extra piquancy.

She rapped the brass knocker and took a depth breath, trying to calm herself.

'Hello.'

For once it was Adrian who opened the front door.

'Hi,' Amanda said.

'Come in, come in. You look gorgeous as always. Love that dress.' He closed the door after her, kissed her on both cheeks and led her into the front room. As seemed to be customary, a bottle of champagne sat in the wine cooler on the table. 'A drink?' he asked.

'Please.' He poured the wine and handed her a glass. 'Natasha told you we've got a surprise for you?'

'Yes.'

'Cheers.' He raised his glass. He was wearing a crisp white shirt and a pair of dark navy trousers with a thin black leather belt.

'Cheers.' Amanda followed suit.

'Sit, please,' he said, arranging himself an armchair. Amanda sat on the sofa.

'Where's Natasha?' She had asked the same question about him four days previously. Was Natasha downstairs, bound and spread on the rostrum, her head sealed in a rubber helmet?

'She's just making some final preparations,' he said. 'You've never played these sort of games before, have you?'

'No.'

'Do you enjoy them?'

'I thought that much was obvious.'

'Sex is a strange thing. When you're involved in it it's like a drug. The better the feeling, the higher you get, the more of it you want. Something takes over, drives you on. The trouble is that after you come down, when you're staring normality in the face again, you can regret what you've done.'

Amanda smiled. 'If that's a roundabout way of asking me if I regret last time, no I don't. I wouldn't be here if I did.'

'Good. In that case I'd like you to take your dress off now, Mandy. If you wouldn't mind.' He said it as casually as if he was asking her to take off her coat and, strangely, that tone excited her.

Amanda sipped her champagne, then put the glass down and got to her feet. She stood directly in front of Adrian and reached behind her back for the zip of the dress. It sang as she pulled it down. She extracted her arms from the sleeves and wriggled the dress over her waist. It fell to the floor.

She had chosen her underwear as carefully as she had before. She wore a black lace waspie corset around her waist that emphasised its hour-glass shape. The lace was delicate and transparent. Long black suspenders snaked over her hips, only four this time, to support very sheer and shiny black stockings. The top of the waspie nestled under her breasts. She was not wearing a bra. Tiny black lacy panties, no more than a triangle of lace covering her mons held in place by thin black satin straps, completed her outfit.

'How lovely,' he said, studying her body intently.

'You approve?'

She turned around. The straps of the panties emerged from the top of the cleft of her buttocks. There they diverged forming a V-shape across her bottom. The strap between her legs had worked its way into her labia and hid little of her sex. She had decided on a pair of the black patent leather shoes, with precipitous heels, and knew that they shaped her legs, pouting her buttocks out from the top of her thighs and firming the muscles of her calves.

'Most definitely.' He reached forward and stroked the jet black welt of the stocking. His hand moved up to the soft, creamy flesh above it, then back to the shiny nylon. 'Such a contrast,' he said.

'What do you want me to do now?' Amanda's body was buzzing with excitement. Being semi-clothed in a bedroom was one thing, but standing here in the sitting room with a comparative and fully dressed stranger was something completely other. It felt wicked.

'Bend over,' he said. 'I'd like to look at you carefully.'

'Like this,' Amanda said boldly, spreading her legs apart then bending over and grasping her ankles. She remembered the last time she had done this for Greg and the disappointment it had led to. Whatever else happened tonight she was sure she wasn't going to suffer that fate.

'Perfect,' he said. He shifted forward until he was on the edge of the chair and inserted his fingers under the strap of the panties, gently pulling it out from the crease of her sex and arranging it carefully to one side so it would not fall back.

Amanda thought he was going to touch her. Her clitoris pulsed wildly, as if trying to attract attention to itself, and she was sure her labia had opened to reveal her vagina, but he drew back.

'All right, straighten up,' he said. 'I'm going to have to blindfold you now.'

'What?'

'It is necessary.'

'What for?' Amanda had done things in the last days that many would regard as outrageous, but she wasn't sure she wanted to do this.

'Trust me, Mandy,' he said softly. He got to his feet and stroked her upper arm. Amanda could see the front of his trousers was distended. He followed her eyes to the bulge. 'You see what you've done to me?'

'I want to *see* more of it,' she said.

'You will. But first you have to do as I say.'

Mandy hesitated. She could put her dress back on and go home but she knew she wasn't going to do that. She didn't want her adventure with the Chrystals to end. But if that were the case she would have to put her misgivings aside.

Adrian went to a small metal box on the mantelshelf and took out what appeared to be a strip of black silk. As he brought it closer Amanda could see two thick black pads had been sown into it in the middle of its length.

'Well?' he said.

She nodded her head curtly and closed her eyes. She clearly had no choice if she wanted to stay.

Adrian fitted the silk over the bridge of her nose. The pads pressed against her eyelids. The silk was knotted tightly around her head, increasing the pressure, and cutting out even the faintest penumbra of light.

'Can you see anything?' he asked, knowing full well she couldn't. He had worn the same blindfold many times.

'No.'

'Good. Now I'm going to take your hand. Don't worry. I won't let you bump into anything.'

'Are we going to the cellar?' Amanda was worried about going downstairs with the blindfold on.

'No.'

His fingers laced into hers. He pulled her forward. The soft carpet gave way to the hard wooden floor of the hall. In her mind's eye she saw herself being led across the corridor, in her corset, stockings and panties, like some ritual sacrifice prepared for the altar of sex. She heard a door being opened. She was pulled through into another room, where she had never been before. Her shoes fell on carpet again. Who was there? Whose eyes were watching her? Some instinct told her it was not just Natasha and Adrian. The idea of unknown eyes examining her minutely made her feel suddenly defenceless. She shivered, her flesh breaking out in goose pimples.

Adrian led her forward a couple of steps, then let go of her hand. 'Stay where you are,' he said gently.

Amanda listened. It was extraordinary how being deprived of one of the senses seemed to increase the sensitivity of all the others. She could feel every inch of the tight waspie constricting her flesh, and the long suspenders stretched tautly over her long legs. The black strap of her panties had slipped back into her sex as she walked and was rubbing against her clit.

She listened for any sound that might give her a clue as to who else was in the room. She could hear breathing, but the noise of her own breath made it difficult to distinguish any detail.

One thing she was sure about was that she could smell a flowery perfume, which was not the one Natasha had used before. It was also a scent she recognised, though she could not place where or when she had smelt it before. Of course, it might just be that Natasha had changed to a new scent, but most women stuck with a single perfume and she thought that unlikely. Did that mean there was another woman in the room?

She heard clothes rustling. In the heightened condition of her senses the sound was magnified. She heard the sharp metallic click of a belt buckle and imagined Adrian was getting undressed.

She was right. She felt the heat of his body coming up behind her and his erect penis nudged her buttocks.

'Two steps forward,' he said with his hands clutching her shoulders. 'Now turn round.' As she turned he pushed her back slightly and she felt the edge of something soft against the back of her knees. 'Sit,' he said.

Amanda obeyed.

'You're sitting on the edge of a bed,' he said. 'Now move to your left and lie on your back.'

Again Amanda obeyed. The linen was newly washed and smelt faintly of soap powder.

'What now?' she said.

Adrian did not answer.

Amanda listened again. There was no movement. Suddenly she started. A hand was brushing her thigh. It moved up over her stomach and glanced lightly against her breasts, one after the other.

'Move to your left again, so you're in the middle of the bed,' Adrian said, 'then roll onto your side.' His voice was precise and detached.

Amanda did as she was told. Though she had never fantasised about anything remotely like this she found it exciting. Her nipples were puckered so tight it felt like they had been knotted and there was a slick of wetness between her legs, the strap of the panties already soaked.

The hand caressed her face. It moved across the silk of the blindfold and Amanda could feel it against her eyelids. A finger traced the contours of her lips. She opened her mouth and the finger delved inside. Amanda raised her tongue and

116

the finger pushed against it, then ran along the edge of her teeth. Another finger joined the first.

'Suck them,' Adrian said. His voice had changed direction. He was closer to her now, standing, or so she thought, behind her head.

Amanda sucked at the fingers. She knew instinctively they belonged to a woman. Was Natasha kneeling on the bed beside her?

The fingers departed. A weight moved across the mattress. She felt the heat of another body behind her. An arm wrapped around her side, a hand cupping her right breast, as a body crushed into her back. It was a woman. And she knew at once it was not Natasha; the breasts that squashed into her shoulder blades were too heavy and fleshy. That realisation produced a huge surge of feeling. She had allowed perfect strangers the free use of her body. Now she was going one step further, being touched intimately by a woman she had never even seen. It was so beyond anything she had done before, so wicked and debauched, it inflamed her.

A hand was snaking over her belly, pushing under the tiny panties and probing between her legs. As the middle finger of the hand made contact with her clitoris Amanda groaned. It had never felt so sensitive. The finger moved up and down, dragging the little nut of flesh with it, and producing ripples of sensation that made Amanda close her eyes with delight, wallowing in the pleasure of her depravity.

'Oh yes,' she said.

'I told you to trust me.' Adrian's voice sounded smug. He could see the way Amanda's whole body was suddenly suffused with pleasure.

Amanda wriggled back against the woman, pushing her buttocks into her stomach. The finger did not lose its rhythm. It moved relentlessly up and down, the wetness Amanda had produced lubricating its passage.

'Oh, that's so good,' Amanda said, 'don't stop.' She didn't

know this woman, or what she was capable of, but she hoped desperately she would not stop what she was doing.

'She's not going to stop,' Adrian said.

It appeared that everything that had happened, the way she'd been made to bend over in the sitting room, the way Adrian had examined her then blindfolded her, had aroused her despite her misgivings. But the fact that a stranger was lying naked behind her, using her body shamelessly, threw her arousal into another gear. Her body was primed and ready, an orgasm blossoming faster than it ever had before.

'Don't stop,' she repeated, her voice strained and husky. She felt the woman's mouth sucking at her neck and her other hand plucking at her nipple, pinching it quite hard. The two sensations united with the unbelievable pleasure from her sex. Whoever she was, she knew exactly what to do to make Amanda's pleasure complete. In seconds she was on the brink, then plunging over it, her orgasm coming in a spiral of pleasure that curled tighter and tighter until her body could take no more.

The finger withdrew.

They gave her a minute for the orgasm to pass, watching her body as it trembled and shook, her breath coming in hurried pants.

And then it was time for the next stage. Adrian, the ring master of this particular circus, nodded.

Amanda felt a weight settle on the bed in front of her. A hand caressed her cheek, then lips brushed her mouth. She knew instinctively they belonged to Natasha. She felt the brunette's breasts brushing against her own.

'Natasha?' she said.

The lips sealed her mouth, kissing her deeply as the woman behind her began stroking her body, her hand moving down her side to her legs, caressing her thighs above and below the stockings. Arms folded around her until the two women encased her, making her the meat in a sandwich.

Natasha's tongue plunged into her mouth. Hands slid

over her body pulling her on to her back, opening her legs, squeezing her breasts, invading, none too subtly, the passages of her body, fingers sliding into her on the flood of her own juices. Two mouths sucked at her nipples. Two mouths licked and sucked and kissed at her belly and her thighs, as she felt her legs lifted into the air. Teeth pinched and nipped the flesh of her thigh. A tongue licked her clitoris then snaked down her sex to her vagina, pushing up into her, her sense of touch enhanced by the fact she could not see.

She was coming again. Her whole body was trembling. Every part of her was alive with pleasure, every inch of flesh responding to sensations she could hardly believe. She didn't have time to think, to analyse, to work out who was doing what. All she could do was feel.

Like the main spring of a watch, she felt her body being wound into another orgasm. She came sharply, almost painfully, but even before she'd uncoiled from that extreme another was winding up in her, stronger and more acute.

She did not know how long it went on. She tried feebly to return the caresses but as she groped around her hands were pushed away.

Eventually they let her rest again. This time she was gasping for air. They watched as she got her breath back, her chest heaving.

Then they started again. This time it was less frantic.

Amanda felt her legs being lowered. The tiny panties, pushed to the side until now, were drawn down and discarded, then her legs spread open again. She sensed one of the women kneeling between them, her arms wrapping around Amanda's thighs, her mouth pressing into her sex. Despite everything that had gone before, the first touch of her tongue, its tip parting Amanda's labia and finding her clit, produced an enormous wave of feeling. Amanda moaned loudly. The tongue was delicate and hot. It prodded her clitoris from side to side as Amanda felt fingers, three at least she thought, plunging into the liquid centre of her vagina. She reared her hips off the bed reflexively, knowing instantly that this treatment would make her come once more.

But that was not all. A weight shifted beside her. Amanda felt a woman straddling her shoulders. At once the wetness and softness of the woman's labia enveloped Amanda's mouth.

Amanda reacted eagerly. At last she was being given a chance to act as well as react. She raised her head and kissed the proffered sex as if it were a mouth. The lack of pubic hair made her think it was Natasha who knelt above her, but she supposed it was possible the other woman was shaved too. She raised her hand and guided it up over the woman's buttocks and down until she located the mouth of her vagina, pushing two fingers up into it. A wonderful pulse of pleasure was her reward, the woman's sticky wetness closing around them.

Amanda's tongue explored the crease of the woman's sex. She was sure it was Natasha now. She could smell the scent she had used before, a dab of it, no doubt, applied between thighs. She found her clitoris and squashed it back, feeling her body start at the sudden assault.

It was exactly what she had experienced before, her mouth and tongue fast against the deliciously pliant and melting wetness of a woman, just as another mouth was fast against hers, except this time the connection was threefold, three women joined in a circle, not two. It didn't seem to matter. Everything she experienced, every little tremor of feeling, every *frisson* of pleasure, she could replicate exactly with her own mouth. As she felt her body readying itself, yet again, for another explosion of feeling, so she could feel Natasha's do the same, driven by the same needs and desires.

She wasn't even sure who came first. Natasha's sex seemed to open above her, pressing down on her mouth, moulding itself to her face. She felt Natasha's body tense and her sex contract and heard her gasp. But at exactly the same time her own body was tensing too, her sex contracting around the fingers that invaded it, and her clitoris dancing against the tongue that batted it from side to side and she was coming too, as hard and poignantly as she'd come before. The blindfold concentrated everything. She realised that. She didn't have to close her eyes to experience the extra thrills of passion. They were already closed, the darkness absolute, a blank screen on which to play the images that had haunted her for days, vivid pictures of her sexual encounters mixed inextricably with a mind's eye view of herself now lying with two women on a bed she'd never seen, a mélange that made her climax once more.

She came out of it in time to feel a weight shifting again. This time she was being moved. She was rolled on to her stomach and brought up to her knees, strong hands pulling her by the hips. She sensed legs stretching out on either side of her. A hand was pushing her head down. Her lips touched a woman's thigh. She kissed it and worked her mouth up until she could centre it between the woman's legs. This was definitely not Natasha. The pubic hair that covered the woman's sex was thick, her labia much more meaty.

It didn't matter. She licked the long slit of the woman's sex enthusiastically. It tasted different. It smelt different, the perfume she had recognised earlier mixed with the musky odours of sex.

She heard the woman moan as her tongue found her clitoris. It was bigger than Natasha's, a long lozenge of flesh. As she stroked it with her tongue the woman's thighs squeezed inward, trapping her face. But that did not prevent her moving her tongue and she continued her work, pushing the clit up and down and feeling the woman respond. It did not prevent her pushing her fingers under the woman's thighs either and penetrating her cunt with two of them. She remembered what had been done to her last time and pushed another finger up into the woman's anus, producing another, louder moan. The woman was near to her climax. Very near. By a sort of osmosis Amanda could feel it. The silky wet flesh inside her vagina was seething, her clitoris throbbing wildly. The woman arched her body off the bed and spread her thighs apart again making it easier for Amanda to ply her clit.

And then she screamed and her whole body shuddered. Her thighs clamped together again around Amanda's cheeks and she pushed her sex hard against Amanda's chin, her body stretched out over the bed, every muscle rigid.

A thaw set in. The woman's body melted.

'Stand her up.'

It was Adrian's voice. Oddly it came as a shock to Amanda. She had simply forgotten about him. She felt the women pulling her to her feet. She had come so much her knees were weak and she staggered as she stood up.

'Over here.'

They walked her forward.

'You're not finished, are you?' he said.

'No. No.' It was true. She realised she was far from finished. Her orgasms had been wonderful, but they had left her with a need neither woman could satisfy.

'Come here.' She felt him take her hands and pull her forward. He was sitting on a chair. She parted her legs to straddle his lap, then felt his hands on her thighs, forcing her down. His cock butted against her labia.

She heard a noise behind her. It was the door opening. It closed again.

She barely registered it. She groped behind her buttocks and caught hold of his cock. It was rock hard. She positioned it in the centre of her sex and slid down on it. The feeling of his phallus plunging into her was exquisite. She threw her head back and almost fell backward, but Natasha caught her, pressing her naked body into her back.

She felt Adrian reach up to the silk that covered her eyes. It loosened. He pulled it away. She blinked. After so long in the dark it took a minute for her eyes to adjust. The light in the room was dim. She looked into Adrian's face then looked around. Natasha was naked apart from a pair of red, stiletto-heeled shoes. There was no one else in the room. The other woman had gone.

'What have you done to me?' she said. Her sex was gripping his penis so hard she thought she might crush it.

'What you wanted,' Natasha said.

'And now it's my turn,' Adrian said, bucking his hips to take his cock deeper into it.

'You want me,' Amanda said unnecessarily. It was obvious he wanted her. Wasn't the evidence buried deep inside her body? She wriggled down on him, grinding her hips so her pubic bone was forced against the base of his cock. She felt him pulse. She felt something else too. Natasha's hand was snaking down over the lace of the waspie. It insinuated between the cleft of her buttocks. Her finger nosed into the small, puckered crater of Amanda's anus.

'No,' Amanda cried. She wasn't sure she could take it. Being penetrated front and rear by fingers was one thing, but with the breadth of Adrian's cock already buried in her vagina she wasn't sure there was room for anything else.

But Natasha did not hesitate. The wetness from Amanda's body had run down over her buttocks. Her anus was moist. As her finger pressed forward it offered little resistance, a token barrier quickly demolished.

'Oh, God!' Amanda cried. She had never felt anything like this. A wave of pain turned to the most buzzing, excruciating pleasure. She thought she had been in control, ready to use her cunt to milk Adrian's spunk out of him, giving back some of what she'd got. But this new development plunged her back into pure indulgence. She could do nothing but feel, especially when she realised that not only was Natasha's finger moving inside her but that she was using her other hand to burrow down between their bodies and search out Amanda's clit.

After so long without the ability to see it came as an added thrill to be able to turn and look at the naked woman. Their eyes met at the instant she felt Adrian's cock spasm inside her, jerking against her own vagina and his wife's finger. As he bucked his cock into her, wanting to get his jetting spunk as deep as it would go, his hands crawling at her hips, her orgasm exploded too, sending her into paroxyms of passion. Each orgasm she'd experienced tonight had seemed to be the best. And this was no exception.

'Another glass?' Adrian asked.

He was holding up a tear-shaped bottle of Otard XO.

'Please.' Amanda needed it. As she held up her glass she realised her hand was shaking.

Adrian poured the amber liquid into the brandy balloon. He offered the bottle to his wife who also accepted.

It was dark outside and they had drawn the heavy curtains over the large window at the front of the sitting room. Amanda and Natasha sat side by side on the big, comfortable sofa.

'I feel wonderful,' Natasha said. She sipped the brandy then put her feet up, resting her head against the side of Amanda's thigh. They were all wearing fluffy white towelling robes.

'I feel wonderful and shattered,' Amanda said.

Adrian sat in the big leather armchair at the side of the marble fireplace that dominated the room, its iron grate currently full of dried wild flowers.

'As long as you had a good time. I know I did,' he said, grinning.

'And who was the mystery guest?'

'If we tell you it wouldn't be a mystery would it?' Natasha said.

'Is there any reason I shouldn't know?'

'She's shy. That's all,' Adrian said.

'Shy wouldn't be how I'd have described her,' Amanda said.

'All right, embarrassed I suppose would be a better word. We've been friendly with her long time but she gets embarrassed with anyone else. That's why we use the blindfold.'

'That, and the fact that it's very exciting,' Natasha said. She reached up to the collar of Amanda's robe and pulled her down by it, so she could kiss her lightly on the lips. 'Very exciting.'

'Listen, Mandy, we wondered if you'd be interested in coming to a party with us.'

'A party?' Amanda looked puzzled.

'An orgy, darling, *une partouze.*'

'What sort of orgy?' Amanda had a vision of forty naked people rolling around on the floor together, heaving buttocks and heaving bosoms, all vying for attention.

'Oh, very discreet. It's a friend of ours.'

'From *Contacts*?' Amanda asked.

'Yes, as a matter of fact. We answered an ad to go to the first party he ever held. It was fun.'

'So, what happens?' Amanda had thought she was totally replete, but her body managed a pulse of excitement as her imagination ran riot.

'Oh, he's very rich. Got a beautiful house. Swimming pool. Big garden. Lots of bedrooms. Lots of booze and good food.'

'And if you see someone who you fancy then you can take them upstairs. There're no rules. Men or women.'

'I thought orgies were where everyone did it together.'

Adrian laughed. 'Oh, that happens too. There's one room for the exhibitionists. But usually we've tended to stick together, find another couple, or a couple of girls, something like that.'

'There is one rule though. It's couples only.'

'Couples?'

'You'd have to bring your husband along.' Natasha said.

'Do you think he'd be interested?'

'You must be joking! Greg isn't interested in sex. That's why I got into all this.'

'Really?' Natasha looked genuinely surprised.

'He used to be. But not now.'

'There'll be some very beautiful women,' Adrian said.

'Including me,' Natasha said. 'I'd love to fuck your husband.'

'A sort of quid pro quo?' Amanda joked.

'Exactly. Don't you think he'd be interested in me?' She raised one leg in the air. The towelling robe fell away and Amanda glimpsed her carefully coiffeured mons.

'I wish I could say yes.' It was true. The sort of event they had described had set Amanda's pulses racing. The idea of a room full of men, like Phil and Adrian, or women like Annie and Natasha for that matter, all available for sex, seemed almost too good to be true. What she had experienced with Annie and Phil, and now in this house with the Chrystals, was exactly that. It was sex for sex's sake. With no emotional connotations or complications. Pure, unadulterated sex. That was, she knew, why she had got so much pleasure from her experiences. She did not want love. She wanted lust. 'He's just not into sex these days.'

'Have you thought that he might be getting it elsewhere?' Natasha asked. She put her leg down but made no effort to rearrange the robe.

'It's possible, but I really don't think so. I'm sure I'd see the signs. He's a workaholic. He lives to work. We used to have wonderful sex. He knows if he wants it again I'm available. He just doesn't want it.'

'Pity.'

'You're telling me. I'd really love to come. Talking of Greg, I better get a cab. I'm going to be late.' Amanda got to her feet, easing Natasha's head back on to the seat of the sofa. The brunette lay there looking up at her.

'That's a pity too,' she said.

Chapter Seven

It started to rain on Friday evening and rained all night. It hadn't stopped as Amanda parked the car and carried in the groceries from the weekly supermarket expedition.

As she reached her front door, Maggie's door opened.

'Hi.'

'I thought you were going away.'

'Came back early. Do you want a coffee?'

'Love one. Just let me put these inside.'

Minutes later they were sitting around Maggie's coffee table with a pot of filter coffee and two delicate bone china cups. Maggie always had the best coffee. There was a coffee shop next to her office and she got fresh supplies regularly, insisting on buying small quantities. The fresher the coffee the better it tasted. At least according to her.

'So?' she said, raising an eyebrow and grinning.

'So?' Amanda said non-commitally.

'You had a good time?'

'You know I did.'

'Come on, give me all the gory details.'

'What is this, vicarious living?'

'Exactly. My supply of men seems to have dried up.'

'And what about women?'

'Naughty. I thought that was an issue we were going to treat with taste and delicacy.'

'Sorry.'

'So what happened?'

Amanda told her the full unexpurgated version. Maggie looked opened-mouthed.

'So you never actually saw who it was?' she said when the tale was told.

'No. I never did. But I didn't believe them.'

'What do you mean?'

'They told me she was embarrassed.' She'd thought a lot about what Adrian had said and it didn't ring true. A woman who was embarrassed about having sex with strangers was hardly likely to have got involved with Adrian and Natasha in the first place. 'I don't believe it.'

'What, then?'

'Don't know.'

'It sounds plausible to me.'

'Anyway, that was not all. They asked me to go to a party. What was Natasha's word for it? *Partouze*.'

'From the French *partout*. Everywhere.'

'Really? How appropriate.'

'Did you accept?'

'Couldn't.'

'Why not?'

'Because it's couples only. No singles. I understand why. Don't want any of the men running off with a single woman I suppose. Breaking up the happy home.'

'And you couldn't take Greg?'

'Of course not. You know what he's like.'

'I know what you've told me. That's different. He's an attractive man.'

'What does that mean?'

'It means that if a beautiful young blonde came up to him and asked him if he'd like to take her upstairs for a fuck what do you think he'd say?'

'I think he'd run thirty miles in the opposite direction.'

'Oh.' That seemed to stop Maggie in her tracks.

'Don't you think he would?'

'I don't know him like you do. I know the problems you've

been having and I think that happens a lot with married couples. But then suddenly, bingo, the guys run off with some daffy blonde from the office. You haven't lost interest in sex. Why should he? He used to be very good at it, according to you. See, I think sex is a bit like a volcano. It erupts in the first place and makes a huge crater, then the fire goes out of it and it lies dormant. But sooner or later it's going to explode again and often the second explosion is bigger than the first. That's what's happened to you, isn't it?'

'The only thing that interests him is the business, Maggie.'

'OK. So why don't you try a little experiment?'

'What sort of experiment?'

'Tell him you've been invited to a party by a couple of old friends you haven't seen for years. But don't tell him what sort of party it is.'

'How can I do that?'

'Just do it. There'll be drinks and food no doubt. Just like any other party.'

'And what happens when people start taking their clothes off?'

'Plead ignorance. If he thinks it's disgusting you can leave. Just tell him you had no idea it was going to be that sort of party and you're as shocked as he is and storm out. But what if he isn't so disgusted after all? Say he's approached by some lovely young thing who he happens to find irresistible.'

'Natasha's already offered.'

'There you are, then. Natasha's gorgeous. I certainly can't resist her.' Maggie laughed.

Amanda sipped her coffee. 'It might work.'

'What have you got to lose? At worst you have a nice drink, a nice meal and come home early. On the other hand it might be just the sort of fillip he needs.'

'Get the volcano erupting again.'

'Exactly. Make sure you brief Natasha and Adrian. She can pretend she's an old schoolfriend or something.'

'Good idea.'

'Well?'

'As you say, what have I got to lose? Thanks Maggie. It's a brilliant idea.'

'Call them now, if you like. Their number's in the book by the phone on the hall table.'

'I will.'

Amanda got up and went into the hall. There was a small table by the front door right next to a Victorian coat stand. She looked up the number and dialled, leaning against one of the coats. There was no reply.

The aroma of Maggie's perfume lingered on the garments. And that's when she realised why she'd recognised the scent of the mystery woman on Thursday night. It hit her like a bolt out of the blue. It was Maggie O'Keefe.

'No reply. Just going to the loo,' she shouted through to the kitchen. She needed time to think.

She ran upstairs and locked herself in the bathroom. It explained everything of course. The woman was not shy or embarrassed. She just didn't want Amanda to know it was her. She'd told her that she was going to Manchester on Saturday as part of the strategy.

Amanda's first reaction was anger. She was annoyed with her friend for not being straight with her. But her second emotion was deeper and much more affecting. She felt a surge of lust. Ever since they had brought the subject up she had been unable to stop herself imagining what it would be like to be swept into Maggie's arms.

Now she knew. Intimately.

Her knees felt weak. She sat on the toilet.

The problem was what she did now. Should she go downstairs, kiss Maggie full on the mouth and ask her to take her to bed? God, how wonderful that would be! She'd love to feel those heavy breasts pressing into her shoulders again and that delicious mouth sucking at her sex. She'd love to spread Maggie's legs and kneel between them again and bring her off as she had before, this time knowing who the cries of esctasy belonged to.

But she wasn't sure she could cope with that at the moment. She wanted to examine the implications of having a lover living right next door to her. And above all she didn't want to lose Maggie as a friend.

In fact she realised Maggie had done exactly the right thing. In her position she would have probably done the same. With the Chrystals no doubt willing to help, she had slaked her lust with no consequences for their relationship.

It was up to Amanda now. If she wanted to reveal that she knew the truth she could at any time, and they could try to work out the implications face to face. Or she could remain quiet and simply ask the Chrystals to arrange another session with their mysterious friend. The thought of the latter was exhilarating. She could almost feel the silk being tied over her eyes. But this time the stranger's body would not be an enigma. The flesh she kissed and licked and sucked would be all too familiar.

She flushed the loo and walked down stairs.

'Another coffee?' Maggie asked.

Amanda looked at her. She felt a surge of lust. The temptation to fling her arms around the woman's shoulders and kiss her was almost irresistible. But she managed to resist it. Just.

'Yes, I'd love some more,' she said.

Maggie poured the steaming black liquid.

'Have you thought about what we were talking about last time?' she said. Resisting temptation didn't mean she couldn't play with fire.

'Last time?'

'Whenever it was. About having sex.'

'I'm not with you.'

'What it would be like to have sex with each other?' Amanda said pointedly, looking straight into Maggie's eyes.

The woman stared back, hesitating for a moment before she spoke. 'It wouldn't be a good idea, would it?'

'You're a very attractive woman, Maggie,' she said steadily.

'Sex would get in the way though. I thought that's what you said.'

'I know what I said. Have you ever thought about it, though? I have.' She ran her finger across her bottom lip, then slipped her fingertips down to touch her throat.

'Have you?' Maggie was looking at her warily.

'Of course. You've got such a lovely mouth. I've thought about what it would feel like to kiss it.' Amanda ran her hand down over the front of her blouse. It was no surprise to find her nipples were as hard as buttons. 'And your breasts. I've imagined them crushing into . . .' She was just about to say shoulder blades but thought that might be giving the game away, '. . . mine.' She stroked her hand up and down across her right breast. 'Don't tell me you haven't imagined what it would be like to be with me.'

'I have.' Maggie looked distinctly uncomfortable. 'Of course I have.'

'And?'

'I think I'm frightened of ruining our friendship.' That was the absolute truth. Maggie was regretting what she'd persuaded the Chrystals to do. Not that she hadn't enjoyed every minute of it, but she didn't want her friend to find out and be angry with her. That really might blight their relationship and, she'd found in life, friends like Amanda were hard to come by.

Amanda decided the game was over. 'Better get going. Greg wants his lunch on a Saturday.'

'Let me know how you get on.'

For a moment Amanda wondered what she was talking about. Then she remembered. 'Oh, right, yes I will. I'll call the Chrystals later on. Greg usually falls asleep in front of the telly. Thanks for everything, Maggie.'

At the front door they kissed on both cheeks. Did their lips linger a moment longer than they had once done, or was Amanda's vivid imagination playing tricks with her again?

*　　*　　*

It was Monday evening. Greg was late again, and they had dinner in the kitchen, a steak and salad and a bottle of Rioja. Amanda suggested they had a brandy and Greg poured them two glasses of the Armagnac they'd brought back from their last trip to France. It was a good way to soften him up.

'Oh, by the way,' she said. 'Do you remember me talking about Natasha Chrystal?'

'She sounds like the star of a porno film,' Greg said.

Amanda almost choked on her drink. When she'd recovered enough to speak she said, 'We were at school together.' It was the story she agreed with the Chrystals.

'Oh. Doesn't ring a bell.'

'Anyway, she's invited us to a party on Saturday.'

Amanda had spoken to Natasha on Saturday afternoon and had been carefully waiting for the right moment to broach the subject with her husband. The Chrystals were delighted with the plot Maggie had hatched and promised to play their part.

'This Saturday?'

'Yes. You're free, aren't you?'

'I suppose so.'

'Don't sound so keen.'

'What sort of party is it? I mean, who's going to be there? Is this girl married now?'

'Yes. But it's not at their house. It's a friend of their's. He's loaded apparently. She says it's a real bash. Champagne, caviar, lobsters, oysters. The works.'

'Sounds a bit odd.'

'Why?'

'Why are they asking us to someone else's party?'

Amanda hadn't got an answer for that. 'Oh . . . I guess . . . I mean this man's a bit of an eccentric apparently,' she said thinking on her feet. 'He likes to meet new people. He's always asking them to bring friends along.'

'And she thought of you after all these years.' He sounded deeply sceptical.

'Actually I bumped into her in M&S a couple of weeks ago. Didn't I tell you?' She was safe there. Greg rarely remembered anything she said.

'No.'

'I suppose that's what gave her the idea. It's a really big house apparently.'

'Where?'

'Bishop's Avenue.'

'Hampstead?'

'Yes.' She knew that would peak Greg's interest. He had worked as an estate agent before he moved into property finance and was always fascinated by poking around the houses of the wealthy.

'Well, we'd better go then. Never say no to a glass of champagne. Come on we'd better get to bed.' He got up and walked towards the stairs.

There was a time in their relationship when such a statement would have meant only one thing. But not now.

'You've got an early start, have you? Amanda said with certainty.

'Yes. Up at seven.'

She smiled to herself as she followed him upstairs. It was funny, she thought. She had come such a long way in such a short time. From being surprised and even shocked at the contents of *Contacts* to weaving a complicated web of deceit in order to get her husband to attend a full-fledged orgy. But she could still honestly say she had no regrets.

The taxi dropped her in a small, nondescript street in Barnet. She couldn't ever recall going to Barnet before. The row of terrace houses were modern, with large flat front windows and the front doors set back to create a small porch. A path led through the narrow but quite long front garden, colourful shrubs growing between large terracotta paving stones. Amanda rang the door bell.

'Hello.' A man had answered the door.

'I'm Amanda.'

'Of course. Come in, won't you?'

The picture in *Contacts* hadn't lied. Though he was not conventionally handsome he was undoubtedly one of the most charismatic men Amanda had ever seen. His face was rather too long, his eyes too deep set, and his nose crooked with a large bump half way down, but there was something about him that exuded confidence, strength and masculinity. He had short, dark, thick hair. The top two buttons of his shirt were open and Amanda could see a mat of hair on his chest too.

The hall was small and neat with two reproduction Corots on the wall. He led her into the front room where there was a red three piece suite on a pink carpet.

'Would you like a drink? We've got some red wine.' The man seemed perfectly at ease.

'That would be nice.'

'Oh, I'm Dan, by the way.' He extended his hand and Amanda shook it. She felt a tingle like electricity. He walked through into the dining room at the back and poured her a glass of wine. His steps were measured and elegant, every movement of his body a lesson in grace. She didn't know why she didn't just strip her clothes off now and beg for him to take her over the back of the sofa.

'And I'm Georgina.'

A tall, elegant woman walked into the room. She had a cloud of soft, curly auburn hair and was wearing a tight, bright green dress that matched her eyes. It was a cocktail dress with a high neck, full sleeves and a diagonal motif that glittered with glass beads. It looked a little out of place at this time of day. Despite her height she had a rather dumpy figure with small breasts and a thick waist, though her hips were narrow and her long legs slender. She wore tanned coloured tights and low-heeled green leather shoes.

'Pleased to meet you,' Amanda said, shaking the woman's hand. She noticed she wore several gold rings and that her nails were beautifully manicured and varnished bright red.

'Likewise.'

Dan brought two glasses of wine and handed them to the women. He picked his own glass up from a coffee table at the side of one of the armchairs.

'Chin, chin,' he said.

They raised their glasses.

In real life the couple looked more incongruous than they had in the photograph in *Contacts*, perhaps because the white basque Georgina had worn had made her seem altogether more alluring.

This had all been very spur of the moment. Amanda had hidden the magazine away in the lingerie drawer, but out of sight was not out of mind. She had found herself thinking about it every time she passed the chest of drawers. On Wednesday afternoon she finally gave in to temptation and got it out again, lying on the bed and flicking through the pages. Of all the ads, she kept coming back to the photograph of the couple who had specifically excluded the conduct that everyone in the magazine referred to as AC/DC. The man in the photograph attracted her like the invisible pull of a magnet. Perhaps, after so much homosexual sex, Amanda's heterosexual side was trying to assert itself, though if that were the case it was entirely unconscious, since she felt no conscious problem in that area.

Rashly, before she'd even thought about what she was doing, she'd called the couple's voice mail box and listened to their message:

'Hello. I'm Dan. My partner's name is Georgina. We're not married but we share a house and we like to experiment. We're not into couples but if you're a woman looking for an experience on your own, something different, then why not leave a message. We can promise you won't be disappointed. Bye for now. Please speak after the tone.'

And Amanda had found herself doing just that. She was at

this number during office hours only, she told them, wanting to make sure they didn't call in the evening.

They called an hour and a half later. Dan introduced himself. They liked the sound of her voice, he told her. She liked the sound of his. He suggested she came around to their house at five. Just for a chat. Just to get to know each other. He did not explain what role his wife was going to play in the proceedings and Amanda did not ask.

If they hadn't struck while the iron was hot it was possible she'd have thought better of the whole idea and told herself off for being greedy. Saturday night was only three days away after all. But Saturday night might prove to be a damp squib with Greg storming out once he realised what was going to happen. There would be no harm in going over to meet the couple, particularly as Greg was going to be late home anyway.

She was definitely glad she had.

'Have you done this before?' Dan asked. He had dark brown eyes that looked at her with an unwavering stare that she found disarming. Was there anything about him that wasn't?

'Yes,' Amanda said.

'That makes things easier, doesn't it?' Georgina said, sitting down and crossing her legs.

'So, why us?' Dan asked.

'I suppose I was intrigued by your ad. Most couples like to indulge in everything.' She sipped her wine and sat in one of the armchairs.

'Everything?' Georgina said. She wore heavy make-up with a thick foundation, her eyelashes obviously false. Her eyes were carefully shadowed with two different shades of colour and her cheeks were hollowed by blusher. Amanda noticed she wore a gold chain around her ankle under the tights.

'She means AC/DC,' Dan said.

'Exactly.'

'The thing is . . .' Georgina said, then hesitated. Her voice was rather strained and low in pitch. 'It's a bit difficult to explain.'

'Don't bother. It doesn't matter to me.'

'We didn't want to give the wrong impression, that's all,' Georgina said.

'So how did you get into *Contacts*?' Dan asked.

'A husband who's not into sex and a girlfriend who is. She recommended it as a way to save my marriage.'

Dan laughed. It was a bright, warm noise. He had very white and very regular teeth Amanda noticed.

'How exactly?' Dan asked.

'Her theory was that sex usually means an affair. But this way there's no emotional complications.'

'So it's worked.'

'I love sex. I need sex. I feel a lot better since I've been getting it again regularly, if you want the truth.'

'You're gorgeous,' Georgina said. 'Love your mouth.'

'I thought you weren't into AC/DC,' Amanda said.

'I'm not,' Georgina replied with no further explanation.

'So what do you normally do?' Dan continued. 'I mean, do you like to talk it all over first? Then we arrange a time and place.'

'He wants to know if we passed the audition,' Georgina said, smiling.

'I don't know what you want.' However deeply involved she had become in her new way of life it still seemed odd to be able to talk about sex so openly. Odd, but very exciting.

'I like to watch, that's all,' Georgina said.

'That's all,' Dan added.

'Watch you?' Amanda asked.

'Yes.'

'Sounds all right to me.' The thought of being in bed with Dan was creating a knot of excitement in the pit of her stomach. Her sex had already developed a soft, sticky centre.

'You wouldn't find that strange?' Dan said.

'No. I think I'd find it exciting.'

'Do you want to think about it first? I mean, we could

arrange a time next week. I did say we were just going to have a chat.'

'Why don't we try a little experiment,' Amanda said, getting to her feet. 'Why don't you come here and kiss me. I think I'd like that.'

'I'd like that too,' Georgina said.

Dan stood up. He was smiling, the corners of his eyes wrinkling in a way Amanda found delightful.

Instead of letting him come to her she took two steps forward, wrapped her arm around his waist and kissed him full on the mouth, pushing her tongue past his lips. It met his and they danced against each other.

'Nice,' she said, breaking away. She touched Dan's cheek. 'I really don't have to think about anything Dan. You're an attractive man. If you want the truth I'd love to go to bed with you.'

Dan appeared unfazed by this sudden declaration. 'You're very forthright, aren't you?'

'I try to be. It's pleasant not to have to go through all the old routines. If we'd met in a bar I'd have to pretend I wasn't interested in you and you'd have to pretend you didn't want to take me to bed. This way we cut out all the bullshit.' She realised that was absolutely true and was pleased with herself that she had got herself into this enviable position. 'So, where's the bedroom?'

'The first door on the right at the top of the stairs,' Dan said. 'There's a bathroom en suite.'

'Why don't you both sit here for five minutes and finish your wine while I get ready.'

'Sounds interesting,' Dan said.

Amanda was wearing a loose silk shift in a pastel shade of blue. She turned round, presenting her back to Dan. 'Unzip me,' she said.

He undid the short zip. Amanda had come prepared. She pushed the shoulder straps of the dress off her shoulders and let it fall to the ground. She was wearing a navy camisole top and matching high cut French knickers in silk with lace panels over the breasts and at the hips. Her flesh-coloured stockings were held up by a matching suspender belt. Her shoes were dark blue stilettos.

'I wish I could get away with that,' Georgina said wistfully.

'Five minutes,' Amanda repeated.

She walked out of the room, knowing their eyes were following her. At the top of the steep, narrow staircase she turned into the bedroom. It was spacious, the walls painted white. There was a large oil painting on one of them in bold colours, a picture of two naked women standing in an emerald forest, facing each other, their hands clasped together, their large breasts almost touching. In the background, hidden among the trees, a man's face watched them, his expression of rapt attention very clearly portrayed.

The furniture in the room consisted of a large double bed, covered in a burgundy-coloured counterpane, two bedside chests with burgundy lampshades and little else. To one side of the bed was a door leading to a white-tiled bathroom.

Feeling completely wanton, Amanda stripped the counterpane off the bed with the rest of the bedding. The undersheet was white. She lay on her back without taking her shoes off, opened her legs and bent her knees, the sheet wrinkling as she dug her heels into it. There was a mirror on the wall opposite the foot of the bed. The top of the frame hung out slightly from the wall so the mirror was set at an angle and reflected the whole area of the bed. Amanda could see herself clearly. The gusset of the French knickers spread tautly across her sex. She ran her hand over it, pressing the material into her labia, and felt a familiar *frisson* of pleasure.

It was extraordinary, she thought, that she felt nothing but arousal. There was no fear, no embarrassment, not the slightest misgiving. There was a certain smug pride. She was proud of herself for daring to take the initiative and not conform to the sterotypes so often thrust onto women. She had wanted sex. Good sex. Great sex. And, through her own efforts, and with a little help from her friends, she had got exactly that.

She arched her hips off the bed, angling her sex up off the bed, watching it in the mirror. The suspenders strained against the stockings, pulling them taut, the flesh of thighs above the nylon welts creamy and soft. She wondered what other scenes had been reflected in the mirror, obviously deliberately sited for that purpose.

'You look comfortable,' Dan said, standing in the doorway to her right. 'Shall I turn the lights down a bit?'

'Good idea.'

He operated a dimmer by the door and the two bedside lamps weakened.

'Where's Georgina?'

'She'll be up in a minute.'

Amanda straightened her legs. 'Come and kiss me again,' she said, patting the bed at her side.

'You're very demanding,' he said.

'Apparently I am. I've found it gets me what I want.'

He sat on the edge of the bed, leant over and kissed her on the mouth. This time it was his tongue that took the lead. His hand glided down over the lacy panels of the camisole, stroking her left breast.

'You've got a beautiful body,' he said.

He moved his mouth to her neck, then down over her collar bone, covering her flesh with little nibbling kisses. He reached her breasts and one after the other sucked on her nipples through the lace.

'Mmmm . . . nice.'

Then he sat up. He pulled off his socks and shoes, unbuttoned his shirt and stood up to pull off his trousers and pants. His cock was already erect. He wasn't circumcised and his glans was covered by his foreskin. His chest was matted with hair as were his arms and legs.

'I like the look of that,' she said.

'Good.' He knelt up on the bed at her side and ran his hand down her legs, pulling off her high heels one by one.

'I was going to dig the heels into your back to make you try harder,' Amanda said.

'I can assure you that won't be necessary,' he said, grinning.

He kissed her knee. His mouth felt hot. He dragged his tongue up along the nylon until it was playing with the clip of her suspender. His tongue ventured under the nylon, then licked her naked flesh.

'Shall I take you knickers off for you?'

'How kind,' she said mockingly.

He put his hands under the camisole and found the waist-band of the French knickers, pulling then down as Amanda lifted her buttocks off the bed and closed her legs to allow him to strip them off.

'That's better,' he said. Amanda opened her legs again and he stared at her naked sex. 'Do you trim it?' he asked. 'It's very neat.'

She shook her head.

His mouth went back to her thigh. He kissed her flesh, moving up until his mouth was buried in the hollow at the top of her thigh to the right of her sex. She felt his tongue licking it and moaned. Avoiding her sex he moved to the hollow on the left side and gave that the same treatment.

She undulated her hips a little trying to draw attention to her sex. It worked. His hand covered the whole slit of her sex, his palm over her vagina, his fingers curling around her labia and the base of her mons. He pressed it forward forcefully, squashing the soft flesh flat, the juices she had produced squelching against his hand. Then his middle finger delved down into the crease of her sex and found her clit. He tapped it lightly, producing a shock of pleasure.

She watched as he lifted himself over her leg and knelt between her thighs. He used the fingers of both hands to stretch her labia apart, staring into the pink and scarlet flesh he had exposed, the mouth of her vagina winking open. Then he centred his mouth on it and she felt his tongue teasing at her clitoris.

She moaned.

He flicked the little nut from side to side and Amanda felt her body tense, her nerves registering each stroke separately. She angled her sex up at him. He was good at this. Almost as good as a woman. His tongue worked steadily as she felt his fingers prodding at the mouth of her vagina. They penetrated a matter of an inch or so then scissored apart, stretching the pliant flesh. Another wave of pleasure flowed through her.

Momentarily she wondered what had happened to Georgina. Perhaps she'd decided not to watch at all. Not that it mattered. What Dan was doing was quite enough.

Another of his fingers was testing the tension of her anal sphincter. The juices from her sex had run down between her buttocks and it was easy for him to drive a finger in, at the same time as he penetrated right up into her vagina with the other two. She had become used to a woman doing this to her, but Dan felt entirely different. His fingers were bigger and harder and had penetrated more deeply. She found herself wriggling down on them, enjoying how they made her feel.

His tongue was relentless. As the fingers began moving in and out of her his tongue adopted the same rhythm, shunting her clitoris from side to side, each movement producing a wave of sensation, and each wave carrying her higher and nearer to what she now knew would be an inevitable orgasm.

'Wonderful,' she breathed, wanting him to know what she was feeling, as if he hadn't been able to feel it in the way her whole body was quivering at his touch. The word seemed to provoke her more. She felt her body clench, her sex and anus contracting around his fingers, and her clitoris throbbing wildly. Then she was coming, her body rigid, her cunt thrust up against his mouth, waves of raw pleasure shuddering through her.

Immediately he sat up. In an instant he had somehow

grasped her ankles in both hands, pulled them into the air so her legs were forming a giant V and thrust his erection deep inside her, all before her orgasm had leaked away. The effect of this sudden invasion, his cock filling her completely, was extraordinary. It was like coming again, harder and infinitely more profoundly, her original orgasm transmogrified into an explosion of feeling as intense as anything she'd ever felt.

'Oh, Christ . . .' she said when she could say anything at all. 'What a wonderful cock.'

'Thank you, kind lady,' he said, lowering her legs. He pulled out of her. 'But that was only the beginning.'

'Mmmm . . . sounds interesting.'

'Come on top of me.'

'This way,' she said, 'so I can see it in the mirror.' She sat up and indicated that she wanted him to lie with his head at the foot of the bed.

He rolled into position and she straddled his hips, as needy for another orgasm as she had been for the first. Her body appeared to be insatiable. Perhaps she was turning into a nymphomaniac. More likely she was just making up for lost time.

She lowered herself down on him, feeling the heat and wetness of his cock nestling into her labia. She looked into the mirror, as she dropped down on him, watching his erection disappear, swallowed up by her body. Then she took hold of the camisole and pulled it over her head. In the mirror she watched as Dan's hands reached up and covered her breasts, pinching her nipples lightly.

She heard a noise and looked over to the bedroom door. Georgina was standing in the doorway. She was wearing the same white basque she had worn in the photograph in *Contacts* but with tan-coloured stockings. Incongruously, she had a small towel wrapped around her waist.

The presence of a third person in the room while she having sex was still new enough and wicked enough to give Amanda a thrill of pleasure. She wriggled herself down on Dan's cock until she could feel the base of his cock grinding against her inflamed clitoris.

'Come and watch,' she said. 'I told you I don't mind.'

Georgina sat on the edge of the bed. There was a look in her eyes Amanda didn't understand, but in her present condition, racked by extremes of pleasure, she was not in the mood to try and work it out.

'Kiss me,' Dan said, pulling her down until their mouths were locked together. His arms wrapped around her back as his tongue explored her mouth, dancing against hers. Lowering her body like this changed the position of his erection inside her, moving it into new areas, where another set of nerves responded with a new wave of sensation. She moaned, the sound muffled by his tongue.

She struggled to sit up but he would not let her, rolling his chest against her breasts so his hard muscles squashed her nipples.

She felt Georgina's weight moving on the bed behind her. She tore away from the kiss and glanced up into the mirror. Georgina was crouching rather awkwardly behind her. She thought the woman had decided to join in and welcomed that idea.

'I don't mind,' she whispered in encouragement, squirming back on Dan's cock, her sex throbbing and wet. Her first orgasm had left her wonderfully responsive.

Georgina leant forward. Amanda felt the lace of the basque resting against her back as Dan moved his arms down to her thighs, his hands stroking her stocking tops.

In the mirror Amanda saw Georgina's hand pulling the towel away, throwing it on to the floor then leaning forward again. And that is when she felt it. Pressing into her buttocks was not the flat belly of a woman but the heat and hardness of a man's erect cock.

Her body reacted before her mind. She felt a stab of arousal. Then her mind caught up. Georgina was a transvestite. He made a very convincing woman but there was absolutely no doubt that he was a man.

'What are you doing?' Amanda said, knowing full well, the cock nudging down toward her anus.

'Do you want me to stop?' Georgina asked.

Of course she did. She had been buggered before. Greg had done it. She liked it. She even loved it. But two men at the same time? That was too much.

'I can't take it,' she said.

'You can,' Dan said quietly.

They had planned this all carefully. She wondered how many other women had been trapped by this routine. No wonder their ad had been so specific about 'hetero' activities. The trouble was Amanda didn't feel capable of indignation. She was too turned on. She was shocked but her body was determining her response not her mind.

In the mirror she saw Georgina reach out for a little blue jar. A second later Amanda felt something cold and greasy being rubbed into the fistula of her anus.

'You want it, don't you?' Dan said. His hands had gone back to her thighs, rubbing against the nylon.

'I can't take it,' Amanda said but now she was not sure that was true. She felt her body pushing up and down on Dan's phallus, its own needs only too clear.

'Like this,' he said. He bucked up inside her, his cock pulsing. It filled her completely. His right hand moved down to her labia and found her clit, pinching it between his thumb and forefinger. At the same time he raised his head and settled his mouth over her right breast, sucking on her nipple.

'No . . .' she moaned.

But it was wonderful. The three sensations seemed to arc together, her body once again lurching towards orgasm. He pulled his cock back slightly then forced it forward again and again. She had the impression that each new penetration was going deeper, opening her, exposing a part of her body no one had ever been before, where raw, unused nerves sung with pleasure.

And that's when it happened. As Dan pulled out she felt another cock slip past the ring of muscles that guarded her anus and lunge up into her.

A wave of pain engulfed her, her eyes closed, a crimson tide rising through the blackness. She thought she was going to pass out. But then the pain was joined by the most intense pleasure she could ever remember feeling, tight, throbbing pleasure that took her instantly to the brink of orgasm and just as quickly over it. But as her orgasm blossomed she felt the men inside her moving. Dan pushed forward as Georgina pulled back. A perfect double act.

Each new thrust produced pain and pleasure in equal measure, the two so inextricably mixed it was impossible to separate them. The pain was pleasure of a sort. It seared into her, one orgasm immediately replacing another.

She was sweating, sweat running down her forehead and over her cheeks and down between her breasts. Dan's mouth still sucked on her nipple and his finger still flicked at her clitoris and a little voice in her head told her she had two cocks inside her, buried inside her.

Then one of them began to spunk. As they rubbed against each other, separated only by the thin membranes of her body, Dan's cock began to throb. He thrust as deeply into her as he could, arching himself off the bed despite the two bodies on top of him and found his place. His glans jerked and a stream of hot spunk jetted out of him.

Again Amanda had the impression he forced himself into some secret place in her body. She felt every single spurt. They were so hot they seemed to scald her. She wriggled down on him but this produced a whole new set of feelings as the cock buried in her rear was forced higher too.

Amanda's body tensed. As Dan's cock softened, Georgina's ploughed into her more fervently. The transvestite was coming too. But not before Amanda. The heat in her vagina and the flood of wetness and the extraordinary melange of pain and pleasure from her anus were combining to take her yet higher, another inevitable crescendo swelling up in her body.

'Yes, yes, yes,' she said, thrusting her buttocks back and looking up into the mirror. It was a bizarre sight. To all intents and purposes it was a woman who half crouched over her, her legs sheathed in stockings and her body encased in a tight lacy basque. But it was a woman with a cock. And a cock that was exploding, swelling with excitement, stretching Amanda's rear to the limit.

And that was the last straw. Amanda felt her body accelerating to orgasm, driven by extremes of pain and pleasure, her mind reeling, her body shaking, every nerve in her body wanting release.

She did not feel Georgina come. After the sharp shock of orgasm her nerves were so inured she was not capable of feeling anything else. She was vaguely aware of both men pulling out of her and rolling her gently on to her back, but then she turned her head into the pillow and could do nothing more but fall unaccountably asleep.

Chapter Eight

They had decided to take a cab. Greg didn't want to drive as the champagne, he had been assured, would be vintage and abundant. Amanda also wanted to be free to indulge.

Amanda couldn't remember the last time they had been out together on a Saturday night. As Greg worked so hard during the week he liked to use the weekends for rest and recuperation, which meant sitting in front of the television, not going out on the town.

She sat beside him in silence. She was wearing a strapless, bright red dress in a shiny, clinging material into which had been woven thin gold threads that caught the light. The line of her lingerie showed up under the dress, but that was precisely the effect she wanted to achieve. Her shoes were a matching red with a spiky heel and a little gold motif on the toes. The motif was in the shape of a crescent moon.

The exigencies of Thursday, to her surprise, had not left her particularly sore, but had had the effect of creating a seemingly permanent state of arousal. She would swear that her nipples had been hard for two days, and her sex so moist she had had to change her panties two or three times a day.

Sitting in the front room, drinking wine with Dan afterwards, he had explained the circumstances to her. Georgina, or George to give him his proper name, was an old friend. Though a devoted transvestite he was patently not homosexual. His greatest desire was to make love to a woman while he was dressed as a woman, but he'd never found any woman who was prepared to agree. Dan had suggested they take an ad in *Contacts* posing as a couple. The worst that could happen was that Georgina would only be able to watch. But if they managed to get the right woman in the right mood, anything was possible. They had specified in the ad that the women should not be AC/DC so as not to attract women who expected to have sex with a like-minded wife. Apparently Dan's plan had worked. Three women had visited the house and only one had refused.

It was fairly obvious to Amanda why she had found the experience so exciting. There was no doubt in her mind that if she had read an ad in *Contacts* from two men asking for a woman to be shared by them both she would have shied away from the idea. Like a lot of sexually active women, she had imagined what it would be like to be penetrated by two cocks at the same time and indeed had often mimicked the experience by thrusting – and, recently having someone else thrust – fingers or dildoes into both passages of her body simultaneously. But pantomiming the action and actually doing it were two different things.

She would never be able to forget the experience, she knew that. It didn't mean she wanted to do it again. In fact she was sure she didn't. She had begun her quest partly because the lump of a husband sitting next to her in the cab, staring out at the shops as they drove up Hampstead High Street, was not prepared to give her what she wanted most. But there was another reason. She wanted to try women again, real women, not men dressed up for the part. The real exhilaration for her was what she'd experienced with the two couples, the softness and tenderness of a woman followed immediately, or even at the same time, by the hardness and power of a man. That had been wonderful. She shuddered at the thought.

'You all right?' her husband asked as he felt her body quiver.

'Someone ran over my grave,' she said hastily.

Of course, her state of permanent arousal was not all due

to Thursday night. She had been having increasingly wild fantasies about what was likely to happen at the house in Bishop's Avenue. Her mind ran riot. She imagined naked women coupling with men in the swimming pool, Bacchanalian orgies of wine and sex in a huge hall draped for some reason in swathes of white linen and garlands of laurel leaves, tables of food being gorged by hungry mouths, red wine dripping from their lips as male phalluses drove into pumpkins and melons as powerfully as they reamed into glistening wet vaginas, the juice from both mingling into a magic nectar.

She had developed more modern themes too, black-painted rooms where women in leather harnesses were chained to all manner of devices, bent forward or pinned back over chairs and trestles, or suspended from the ceiling, while their genitals were ploughed by every shape and size of phallus, some animate and male, others inanimate and strapped to the loins of some gorgeous female. Men, too, were bound and gagged – as Adrian had been – available for use by any woman, their gargantuan cocks gnarled and veined and glittering with the juices of the women who had used them.

She imagined less complex scenarios too, her mind's eye filling with images of Greg assailed by semi-naked females, their six-inch-high heels raised for him to kiss, their bodies encased in fetishistic lingerie, in patent leather basques, their sexes shaved, their long legs sheathed in glassy nylon. One would kneel over his head and the other over his cock. They would sink down on him together, demanding his obeisance, while she was allowed to watch it all, sitting in a comfortable chair enjoying the view. Having finished with him, having sucked him dry, his tongue sore and his cock shrivelled and useless, the Amazons would turn to her, pulling her down, using her as incessantly as they'd used her husband while this time he was forced to watch. She imagined the horror on his face turning increasingly to fascination, his eyes riveted to her body as the Amazons took it in turns to spread her legs and

151

torment her clitoris while they probed her body with massive dildoes, then demanded she returned the compliment.

The nights were the worse. She'd lain awake unable to shake off the spectres that inhabited her mind, the images getting more and more outrageous, the sex more and more *outré*, memories of what had actually happened to her over the last weeks mixed with fantasies of what might happen.

'Nearly there,' Greg said, interrupting her reverie.

The taxi was pulling into Bishop's Avenue, its large houses divided from each other by big gardens and large fences.

'Devil's Reach, is that right, guv?' the driver asked.

'Yes.'

The house was halfway down the road on the left-hand side, the name stamped into a large brass sign mounted on the concave brick walls that extended out on either side of square pillars supporting wrought iron gates.

A uniformed guard stood in front of the gates, holding a clipboard. He walked over to the passenger window.

'Name?' he asked curtly.

'Landseer,' Greg said.

The guard consulted his clipboard. 'Party of two,' he said, ticking their name. He went back to the gate and swung it open, waving them through, at the same time talking into the radio attached to the lapel of his jacket.

A sweeping driveway led to the columned portico of a modern house, where clearly no expense had been spared by the architect to create an expansive and stylish home. As they got out of the taxi the large walnut front door was opened by a young, pretty girl in a very short, black dress with a low-cut box neckline. The dress displayed her long, slender legs and large, fleshy cleavage. She wore black fishnet tights and suede ankle boots with a very high heel.

'Good evening, Mr and Mrs Landseer,' she said brightly. 'Would you like to follow me?'

They stepped into a vast vestibule, its floor tiled in polished grey granite, its ceiling a dome of Perspex. Underneath the centre of the dome and extending down from it was a silver and gold abstract sculpture, incorporated into which were several water shutes, water bubbling down from the top of the structure to a circular reservoir at its base.

The girl opened the double doors at the far end of the area and a cacophony of music and voices and heat flowed out towards them. The room beyond was large but by no means packed with people, the women all in various haute couture creations, some quite outrageously revealing, while the men, without exception, wore black ties and dinner jackets.

'Drinks are over there,' the girl said, indicating a long bar on one side of the room, staffed by two girls in identical dresses to her own. 'Have a nice evening.'

'Thank you,' Greg said.

The girl turned on her heel and walked back to greet the next guests.

'Pretty,' Amanda said.

'Let's get a drink,' Greg said, ignoring her remark, 'start as we mean to go on.'

They walked to the bar. A large silver bowl had been filled with bottles of Krug champagne crushed into ice. One of the girls behind the bar poured them both a glass and offered them a tray of canapes, Beluga caviar arranged on little circles of blini.

'There's my friend,' Amanda said, spotting Natasha. The brunette was wearing a midnight-blue, full-length evening dress with tiny spaghetti straps, her arms sheathed in long, satin evening gloves in exactly the same colour. Adrian was standing next to her in a white dinner jacket.

Amanda led Greg over.

'Hi, darling,' Natasha said, as they arrived at her side. She kissed Amanda on both cheeks.

'Natasha, Adrian, this is Greg.'

'Hi,' Adrian said.

'But he's gorgeous darling,' Natasha said. 'I hope you'll

save a dance for me,' she added, looking straight into Greg's eyes and shaking his hand.

'I'm not very good at it,' Greg said.

'That's not what I heard,' Natasha said, winking at Amanda.

'Behave, Natasha,' Adrian said. 'Sorry about my wife. She always gets over-excited at these parties.'

'Naturally,' Natasha said, 'otherwise there'd be no point.'

'You haven't met our host, have you?' Adrian asked.

'No.'

'Come on, I'll introduce you.'

Adrian guided them across to a large French window overlooking a patio and large, oval swimming pool, all lit by floodlights. Standing in front of the window was a short, stocky man with a bald head. He was talking to two girls, both long-haired blondes, both wearing dresses that clung to their bodies tenuously, one of them made entirely from white lace. The girl's rather flat breasts and large nipples were visible underneath it, as was the triangular scrap of white silk that covered her mons.

'Josef, can I introduce our friends,' Adrian said.

Amanda held her breath, hoping Josef would not say anything that might give Greg a clue as to what was really going on.

'Of course, of course,' he said. He had a heavy accent that sounded Eastern European.

'This is Amanda and Greg Landseer,' Adrian said. 'Josef Beirmann.'

'My dears, I am charmed you were able to come to my little *soirée*.'

He shook Greg's hand then turned his attention to Amanda. He had bright blue eyes that sparkled with life, and a physical presence that would have been difficult to ignore. His small, podgy hand took Amanda's and brought it up to his lips. 'And you are quite enchanting, my dear. I hope to see a lot more of you later on.' His eyes looked at her steadily, dropping to her bosom and then to her legs. 'A lot more.'

154

Another couple came over and he excused himself, walking across the room to meet their guests, the two blondes on either arm.

'Let's get something to eat,' Greg said. 'I'm starving.'

'See you later,' Amanda said to Natasha.

Natasha smiled and winked. 'So far so good,' she whispered conspiratorily.

The food was laid out in the adjoining dining room, a square of four rectangular tables groaning with dishes. There were oysters, tins of caviar, lobsters and crabs on one, plates of salami, patés, *foie gras*, breads and salads on another, while a third had dishes of hot food, *boeuf bourgignon*, *blanquette de veau*, and a rib of beef complete with a chef to carve it. The fourth table was laid with desserts, fantastic concoctions of mousse and meringue, chocolate in every shape and form, and fruit tarts, glazed and glistening under the lights.

Beyond the buffet a long table had been laid so people could eat sitting down. They walked over to it with their plates of food and sat next to a large woman in a bright violet dress, its plunging neckline framing a truly mountainous bosom.

'Lovely food,' she said. She was just finishing her dessert and had left some whipped cream on her plate. She stuck her finger into the cream and licked it off with her tongue. 'Good practice,' she said, grinning.

'Have you been here before?' Greg asked, after he'd demolished half a dozen oysters.

'Of course. Never miss. My husband would kill me if we didn't.'

'He likes his food, does he?' Greg asked.

The woman laughed. 'That's one way of putting it, I suppose. He certainly likes lots of dishes. And he gets them here. Mind you, so do I. In fact you're quite a dish yourself. Is this your wife or someone else's?'

'He's mine,' Amanda said.

'Very tasty,' the woman said looking into Greg's lap. She

155

got to her feet. 'If you'll excuse me . . . call of nature. See you later, handsome.'

'What was that all about?' Greg said as soon as she was out of earshot.

'She obviously fancied you.'

'Bit blatant, wasn't she?'

'Perhaps she's had rather too much to drink.'

They ate their first courses then went back for *boeuf bourgignon*. Amanda was relieved to see, when they got back, that no one else had taken the large woman's place at the table. She didn't want Greg trying to work out any more loaded remarks just yet.

Bottles of red and white wine had been left on the table and Greg poured the claret. It was an *Haut Brion* that he told Amanda must have cost at least fifty pounds a bottle.

'Where does he get his money, I wonder,' he said.

The beef was delicious but Amanda ate little. She was too nervous. Soon, she knew, the real motive for the party would become apparent and she still hadn't the faintest idea what Greg's reaction would be.

'Look at that,' he whispered, nodding his head to the corner of the room.

A young brunette was standing against the wall. She was wearing a sleek, black tube dress made from tulle and decorated with silver sequins in the pattern of a snake twisting around her body. She had her arms around a much older man, and they were kissing, their mouths squirming against each other passionately. The man had forced his hand round behind her back and hitched the skirt of the dress up well above her buttocks, exposing most of her slender legs. From the position of his arm his hand was obviously implanted firmly between her legs.

'They're getting carried away,' Amanda said, trying to make light of it.

'Great food,' Greg said, still staring at the couple.

'Do you want dessert?' Amanda asked.

'No. Let's go back and mingle.'

They walked back into the sitting room. Most of the guests had eaten and were standing around in little groups, as the waitresses brought around glasses of champagne and brandy on silver trays.

'Ladies, gentlemen,' The booming voice came from Josef Beirmann. 'No speeches, of course. Just to toast our evening. Has everyone got a glass?'

A chorus of 'yes' echoed around the room.

'Then here's to us all, and let the festivities begin.'

At that moment the lights went out and the room was illuminated by the sparks from a dozen sparklers stuck into a large, circular dome that sat on top of a wooden chest. The chest was on wheels and was trundled into the centre of the room by two of the waitresses.

The sparklers glowed brightly, then spat and died. A bank of spotlights were trained on the spot where the chest rested. Slowly the lid began to open. The dome and the spent sparklers clattered to the floor.

'What is all this?' Greg hissed into his wife's ear.

'I don't know,' she whispered back. 'Some sort of cabaret?'

A hand appeared in the opening, then an arm. The lid was pushed up until it was at right angles to the chest, then a man's head emerged. It was completely shaved, his pate shining under the lights as though it had been oiled. His face was strong and rugged with a large straight nose and a square jaw. Gradually he straightened up. Like his head the rest of his body was hairless and oiled too, his muscles firm and well defined.

As his pelvis came into view above the top of the chest some of the women gasped. The man was quite naked except for a large rubber phallus held by a harness of tight elasticated straps over his own cock. The phallus was as big as a marrow, but moulded to look like the real thing, the acorn shaped glans at the top, with a distinct ridge under it, and the rest of the shaft distressed to look as if it were gnarled by veins. There was even a rough scrotum, hanging between the man's legs and covering his own.

Amanda looked sideways at her husband, expecting some sort of reaction from him. He gave her none. His mouth was gaping open and his eyes were rooted to the spectacle.

The naked man jumped out of the box. He took the phallus in his hand and began to wank it, bucking his hips up and down at the same time, his muscles dimpling the side of his buttocks. Another hand emerged from the chest. It was obvious female, the nails varnished a ruby red. A second hand appeared, wavering around the first like a dancing snake. Slowly, a head appeared, also completely shaved and oiled. The woman had a round face with a small nose and delicate features, her eyebrows also plucked out. Despite the lack of hair she was a very beautiful woman.

As she straightened up her naked breasts came into view. They were large and very round and seemed to defy gravity, sitting high on her chest like two melons. More extraordinary, though, was the fact that each of her large, dark brown nipples were pierced by a large gold ring. Hanging from the rings was a thin gold chain, looping down between her breasts.

Amanda felt her own nipples pucker instantly. Her sex throbbed strongly and she had to suppress a moan. Some of the other women did not, and there were several gasps and groans from the female contingent.

The girl climbed out of the chest. Like the man she was completely naked and her whole body had been oiled. As her pubes came into view Amanda could see that they too had been shaved, and the girl's labia were as smooth and shiny as the rest of her body.

The man turned to face her, closing the lid of the chest, and then lifting her up on top of it. Instantly the girl jack-knifed her legs into the air like an acrobat, then slowly scissored them apart, at the same time turning herself so that everyone could see her hairless labia.

As soon as she had completed a circuit of three hundred and sixty degrees the man caught hold of the girl and pulled her towards him. He gathered her into his arms while she wrapped her legs around his body and crossed her ankles in the small of his back.

Amanda watched as the head of the enormous phallus nosed into her labia. For a moment she thought he was going to try and force the whole thing into her but he didn't. Instead he used his hips to move it up and down the slit of her sex, spreading her labia apart.

Again Amanda looked at Greg. This time he looked back at her. She was expecting shock and anger or outrage. But what she saw in his eyes was excitement. Not for long, however. Greg smiled at her weakly then looked back at the naked couple, not wanting to miss anything.

The girl moaned loudly. The man had centred the tip of the dildo on her clitoris, using his hand to guide it in tiny circles. The girl moved her hand down his back and grabbed one of the straps of the harness that held the phallus in place. Working her way along it she delved between the deep cleft of his rock-hard buttocks. There must have been some sort of clasp buried there because suddenly the harness fell away, the straps hanging loose.

The man still held the phallus in his hand. As he felt the straps give way he pulled back slightly from the girl, tore the phallus off his cock and in one seamless movement sank his erection into the girl's vagina. It happened so fast Amanda only caught a glimpse of the real thing, but as he pulled out of the hairless sex again she could examine it more closely. It was large and very smooth, the ridge of the glans prominent. Below the shaft Amanda could see his large scrotum hanging loosely.

He brought his erection almost all the way out of the woman, until only the tip was still inside her, looking as though it were being kissed by the pursed lips of her vagina, then drove it back up so hard and so fast the girl groaned.

But she moved her hands to his buttocks and dug her long fingernails into his flesh to spur him on.

He hammered into her, a squelching noise coming from them as he thrust forward. Every muscle of his body seemed to be in action, tensing as he powered his cock into her.

Then he stopped for a moment. Holding the girl tightly he swivelled around so he was resting on the edge of the box and she was suspended in mid air, supported by her legs around his back and his arms, and by her sex hooked on to his phallus. Slowly his left hand moved down her back. He pushed it under her buttocks and Amanda could see his finger sliding into her anus, all the way in until the knuckle was hard against her bottom. Meantime his other hand slid between their bodies. Without losing his rhythm he caught hold of the chain dangling from her breasts and pulled it up until it was in front of her mouth. She immediately took it between her lips and threw her head back quite violently, jerking the chain up and pulling on the rings that pierced her nipples.

She did this twice in quick succession. Each time her whole body quivered under the impact of the sort of pleasure that only comes from such intimate pain. Then Amanda could see she had lost control, her body contorted around the man. With one last effort she wriggled herself down on his cock and his finger, then gave a sort of muted squeal as her body shuddered and she came.

Without apparent effort the man took two steps forward, the woman still clinging to his body. He lifted the lid of the chest and slowly lowered her into it. There was a loud plop as his cock disengaged from her vagina. Her mouth let go of the chain. She curled up and he shut the lid before turning to the audience.

There was a girl to his left. She was wearing a strapless white silk dress with an elaborate ruched silk bodice and a knee length skirt. Before she had realised what was happening the man leapt toward her, grabbed her hand and pulled her into the circle of bright light around the chest.

His cock was glistening. Amanda was sure she could see it pulse.

'I choose you,' the man said.

Instead of expressing any shock the girl smiled broadly. She was wearing long white evening gloves and slid her hands down her body, taking his erection in both hands and squeezing it hard between them to a few whoops of delight from other females in the room. The man, in turn, took hold of the front of her dress and pulled it down to her waist in one movement, exposing her rather pear-shaped breasts. Pulling her hands away from his cock he span her around and bent her over the chest, her naked breasts quivering.

Now he attacked the hem of the dress, pulling it up over her buttocks. Amanda could see the girl was wearing hold ups and lacy bikini knickers. The man caught the back of the knickers, pulled them to one side and jammed his cock between the girl's legs. It disappeared, though whether into her front or rear passage it was impossible to see. Whichever it was, the girl's delight was obvious. She wriggled back on him and moaned loudly.

Amanda saw the man tense. It was quite obvious he was coming and his partner was coming too, her moans turning to screams, each of his inward thrusts provoking a higher pitch. Her fingers clawed at the wooden chest as he knocked her body into it. As she came her body went limp. Immediately he pulled out of her, pushing his erection against her buttocks, an arc of spunk erupted from him, spattering down on her buttocks and the rucked up dress.

The spotlights went out and the room was plunged into darkness. After a few seconds lights came on again, the normal room lights but dimmed to such an extent it was difficult to see at first. The box had gone, as had the naked man. The girl in the white dress was sitting on a sofa, her breasts still exposed, a dazed expression on her face.

Amanda looked at Greg, but he was not looking at her. He was staring down at the armchair to his right. A redhead, her hair long and flowing, was kneeing on the floor in front of the chair, her body thrust between a man's knees, her mouth bobbing up and down on his erection.

They had both been too engrossed in the cabaret to notice what had been going on around them. Dotted across the room, men and women had paired off, their clothes disarranged, as their bodies locked together in a variety of positions. Other guests had not been so carried away by the show and continued to drink and talk, watching the rutting couples with varying degrees of interest.

'What is this?' Greg said, finally tearing his eyes away from the redhead's increasingly frantic fellatio.

'I've no idea,' Amanda said, the answer she'd rehearsed.

'Jesus, Mandy, just look around.'

She did. And so did Greg. She could see the expression on his face go through several incarnations. Shock. Anger. Disgust. Then it changed back to what she had seen during the cabaret. Excitement and arousal.

'Did you know this was going to happen?' he hissed at her in a low voice.

'How could I? I've never been here before.' She'd rehearsed that line too.

'What about your friends?' He looked around for Adrian and Natasha but his eyes came to rest on a woman who was bent over the back of the sofa, her dress hitched up around her waist. A man was ploughing into her from the rear, while the woman who had been sitting on the sofa immediately in front of her had twisted around to kiss her on the mouth.

'We've got to go,' he said without much conviction.

'No, you don't.' A young blonde had planted herself in front of them, her long hair brushed out and flowing over her shoulders. Amanda recognised her immediately. She was one of the girls who had been with Josef, the white lace dress displaying her charms. Her accent was American.

'Yes, we do.'

'And miss all the fun? Don't do that. It would ruin my

evening. I wanted you the moment I set eyes on you,' she said, touching Greg's cheek with her hand and moving so close to him that her body was brushing against his. Quite casually she dropped her hand to his crotch and tweaked his cock. 'I'm sure we could have a real good time together,' she said, smiling wickedly.

Greg was literally speechless. Half of him wanted to run, the other half to stay. He looked at Amanda. The blonde followed his eyes. 'Do you want her to come too? Why not? Two's company and three's a crowd but hey, three's much more interesting.' She grasped his arm. 'Please, pretty please,' she said tugging him forward.

Without looking at Amanda, as if in a trance, he allowed himself to be led across the room. She followed, picking her way through the increasingly intimate scenes, as more couples became involved, the startling evening dresses the women wore being stripped away to reveal equally exotic lingerie, glimmering sheer stockings, taut suspenders, basques, suspender belts, and elaborate bras, in every colour and design, lace, silk and satin in abundance. The women had dressed knowing how the evening would end.

The blonde led Greg into the hall and over to the foot of the stairs where she let go of his arm and mounted them ahead of him. Greg hesitated to follow, his eyes staring at the girl's long legs and firm, pouting buttocks under the thin white lace. As Amanda arrived at his side the girl stopped and looked back, realising he hadn't followed her.

'What are you waiting for?' she said. 'You're not scared are you?'

Greg turned to Amanda.

'This can't be right,' he said.

'I don't mind. It's exciting Greg. I'd like to see you with her. I really would. It's a long time since we did anything really outrageous.'

'You don't mind?' He sounded astonished.

'As long as you leave some for me,' she said.

He looked up at the blonde.

'Come on,' Amanda urged, 'Let's live dangerously for once.'

A woman with wavy brown hair had come up behind them. She was wearing a pair of beige hold ups with lacy welts, a pair of yellow high heels and a bra with quarter cups, that rested under her large breasts, lifting them up but not covering the flesh. She wore nothing else. A large, bald man was following her, fully dressed apart from the fact that his black bow tie had been undone.

The woman pushed past Greg then stopped.

'Hey, you're good enough to eat,' she said, turning around to face him, her big breasts quivering. 'Come and find me will you, I'd love a chunk of you.' She kissed Greg on the cheek and ran upstairs, the bush of hair between her legs shielding her sex from view.

Apparently this galvanised Greg. He took Amanda's hand and marched up the stairs decisively. Seeing this, the blonde climbed ahead of them. She turned left into a long corridor and they followed.

The corridor had doors on either side. The first three or four doors were closed. The girl stopped outside the first one that was not and beckoned them in.

The room was decorated in a patterned wallpaper, with matching curtains, the counterpane on the large double bed in the same material, the colour green predominating. The carpet was sea green and the chest of drawers and bedside tables had been sponge-painted in the same colour.

The blonde waltzed over to the bed as Amanda closed the bedroom door.

'God, I'm so turned on,' she said. 'Unzip me sweetie, will you, I've got to get out of this dress.' She was talking to Greg.

He pulled the long zip right down from the nape of her neck to the top of her buttocks. The white lace dropped away. The girl wriggled out of the tiny knickers and jumped on the bed.

'Who's first?' she said, opening her legs. Her sex was covered with a fine pelt of very short, very soft blonde hair that was almost like fur. Her labia were fat and rubbery and pursed like a mouth waiting for a kiss.

Amanda felt a pulse of excitement as she looked at the girl. She would have loved to drop down between her legs and press her mouth to her inviting pussy. But she had already decided, if she managed to get Greg this far, that she would not indulge herself. She had never told him of her lesbian experiences and thought the shock of seeing her with another woman might well scare him off totally. Her plan had been to show him how much fun he could have if he were as adventurous as she had been over the past weeks. Hopefully that one thing would lead to another. Once he had rediscovered sex, who knew where it would end? She might even be able to suggest they went to visit Natasha and Adrian and had a session in the room, even take out their own ad in *Contacts*.

'She's beautiful, isn't she?' she said, coming up behind her husband and wrestling him out of his jacket. He was staring at the girl's body.

'Come on,' the girl said. 'I need it.' She pouted her lips like a little girl who had just been told she couldn't go out to play.

Amanda unbuttoned his shirt. He pulled off his shoes and socks, then his trousers. The girl was beginning to play with herself, her hand rubbing up and down her sex, her hips undulating sensuously.

Greg pulled off his pants. His cock was beginning to grow. Amanda sat on the edge of the bed. 'Come here,' she said. He took two steps towards her. She grasped his cock in her hand and sucked it into her mouth. He moaned.

The blonde scrambled to her knees and came up behind Amanda, looking over her shoulder. The feeling of her body pressing into her back made Amanda shudder. The blonde had small breasts but her nipples were as hard as stone and Amanda could feel her grinding them into her shoulder blades.

'Now me,' the American said.

Amanda pulled back. Greg's cock was fully erect now and wet from the saliva. As Amanda moved over the girl took her place, gobbling Greg's erection into her mouth and sucking on it so hard her cheeks were dimpled. Again, Greg moaned. The girl's hands snaked around his back and she dug her fingernails into his buttocks as she slid her mouth up and down on him.

Amanda watched with fascination. It was an odd experience to see Greg being fellated by another woman. In the old days, when their sex life had been dynamic, she had performed the same service many times. He often came in her mouth, frequently while he had used his mouth on her, *soixante neuf* a frequent part of their sexual repertoire. But like everything else in recent months he hadn't shown the slightest desire to repeat the experience. Now, however, he appeared to have got back some of his old enthusiasm. She hoped it would not flag.

Amanda unzipped the dress. She was wearing a strapless, scarlet-coloured satin basque and champagne coloured stockings with matching panties. She was glad to see Greg watch her, his eyes sparkling with excitement as she stooped to peel the lacy panties down to her ankles.

'Do you remember this?' she asked him, indicating the basque. 'It used to be your favourite.'

'Great,' he grunted, his eyes roaming his wife's body as if seeing it for the first time. 'Love it.'

'And this,' she said. She lay on her back on the bed, spread her legs apart and bent them at the knee. She used both her hands to spread her labia apart so he could see her sex, the mouth of her vagina winking open.

The blonde pulled her mouth away. Greg's cock was hard, every vein prominent.

'Come on, big boy,' she said, rolling over on to the bed beside Amanda and adopting exactly the same position. 'Let's have some fun. You don't mind if I go first do you, hon?' the girl said matter-of-factly. 'I really need it.'

'Be my guest,' Amanda said. 'Come on Greg, I want to see it.' That was true, she discovered.

All his doubts had gone. He climbed on to the bed and knelt between the girl's legs. He brushed his hand against her sex and stroked her thighs. She angled her sex up towards him.

'Want it,' she said. 'Need it.'

Slowly he lowered himself down on her. Amanda could see his cock nosing between her labia. He held it there teasingly, supporting himself on straight arms, his body poised above the blonde.

'Want it,' she repeated.

He rocked his hips slightly so his cock moved from side to side. It was right on the girl's clit. Amanda's own clitoris was responding in sympathy, waves of pleasure coursing out from it. She grasped her left breast and pinched her nipple quite hard, moaning as the resultant rush of sensation seemed to be routed directly to her sex.

Suddenly Greg fell on the girl. He plunged his cock into the tight wet tube of her sex until he could feel the neck of her womb, pulled almost all the way out, then powered back into her. Amanda felt the impact as much as the girl must have done. Her sex clenched. This was like the old Greg, a wonderful lover, strong and hard and indefatigable. She watched as his buttocks drove forward, every muscle working to get him deeper into her.

'Oh, great, great,' the girl muttered rolling her head from side to side. There was little doubt the girl was coming and coming fast. Her hands wrapped around his back, trying to claw at it, but she didn't have the strength. All her energy was concentrated in her burgeoning orgasm. She lifted her legs in the air, then folded them over Greg's back, the deeper penetration this achieved causing her an instant flood of pure pleasure. Amanda saw her body go rigid, every muscle defined, her fingers contorted like the claws of a bird raking his back. Her mouth opened as though to scream but the sound she made was not a scream, but a little mewing noise that barely escaped her lips at all. Then her body turned to jelly, her arms falling back on the bed, her head lolling to one side.

Greg rolled off her. His eyes looked wild. Amanda hadn't seen him with an expression of such unmitigated lust for years.

'Now you,' he said, his voice hoarse. He took hold of her hand and pulled her up. 'From behind,' he said, frantically pushing her on to her knees, then scrambling up behind her.

'Did she feel good?' Amanda said.

'Yes, yes,' he grunted as his cock, slicked with the juices of one woman, slid into the labia of another.

This time there was no delicate foreplay with his glans. Instead he drove into her liquid centre in one seamless movement, taking her breath away.

He had never felt this big, or this hot. His cock was like a poker left too long in the fire. Amanda's sex contracted around it, a contraction so strong it affected her whole body. As he began pounding into her, his belly slapped against her buttocks loudly. There was a squelching sound from her vagina, her copious juices flooding over him.

The American stirred. She rolled on to her side and put her hand out to cup Amanda's right breast. She tweaked her nipple then moved her hand to the other one and did the same. Then she scrambled over to the other side of the bed and opened the drawer of the bedside table. She searched inside and pulled out a large black rubber dildo.

'Got to have more,' she said. 'Josef thinks of everything.'

Getting to her knees she stuffed the tip of the dildo unceremoniously into her sex. There was no resistance. The black rubber disappeared, only the stub end visible. The girl closed her legs, trapping it there.

'Now, what can I do for you?' she said looking up at Greg.

Her hand caressed Amanda's back, then slipped over the curves of her buttocks. As Greg pulled his cock out she curled her fingers around it and squeezed it hard, so hard his glans ballooned out against the tight confines of Amanda's sex. She moaned. It was almost out of her and the swelling had stretched the tender flesh around the mouth of her vagina to produce a beautiful rush of sensation.

The blonde's hand moved up to Greg's nipple, allowing him to stab his cock forward again. As it reached the inner depths of Amanda's cunt the American pinched his left nipple with her fingernails, producing a wave of feeling that caused his cock to swell again. She moved her fingers to the right nipple and produced the same effect.

Amanda was coming. The feeling of his already bloated cock swelling even more was too much for her. It had set off a chain reaction it was impossible for her to control. She felt her sex clench and her clitoris spasm and a rippling wave of passion rolled up from her sex, gathering in every nerve until there wasn't a single part of her body that was not wrapped up in pure ecstasy.

As Amanda felt her body return to her control she fell forward on to her stomach, wrenching his cock from her sex.

'Hey,' he protested. 'What about me?'

'I've got something special in mind for you,' Amanda said. 'Lie down on your back.'

Greg looked puzzled but nevertheless obeyed, his cock sticking up vertically from his belly.

Amanda knelt at his side. 'Will you help me?' she said to the blonde.

'Sure. What do you want me to do?'

Amanda answered by grasping Greg's cock in her hand. She bent forward and pressed her lips to one side of the swollen flesh. She could taste her own juices. The American quickly got the message. Shifting round to the other side of him, she got into the same position, and dropped her head so her lips were opposite Amanda's, their mouths only separated by Greg's phallus.

'Oh yes,' he said, as they started to slide up and down his cock in unison.

Amanda turned her buttocks towards him, the rear suspender of the basque cutting deep into the soft flesh. The American did the same, allowing him a view of the black rubber protruding from her cunt.

'Finger me,' Amanda said, without taking her mouth away, her lips moving against his erection.

'And me,' the American echoed.

He didn't have to be asked twice. His left hand stroked the curves of Amanda's buttocks then eased down into the slit of her sex. His right pulled the black rubber dildo out of the American and replaced it with two fingers. As he drove the fingers of both hands into the vaginas of both women they felt his cock spasm with excitement at what he was doing.

'Great,' he said, screwing his fingers around, feeling their silky wet vaginas where his cock had so recently ploughed. 'God, this is great.'

The American slipped her hand over his chest and grasped his nipple in her fingers again, using her fingernails to pinch it hard. Amanda took the hint and did the same. Again they felt the result, his cock bucking against their lips, throbbing so much now Amanda was sure he was going to come. Clearly the American drew the same conclusion.

'You take it,' she said. She moved her mouth down to his balls, using her hand to make him spread his legs further apart, then dipping her head right down between his thighs and sucking his whole scrotum into her mouth.

Greg moaned. His cock jerked so strongly it pulled right away from Amanda's mouth. For a moment she thought he was going to ejaculate there and then. But he didn't. She managed to grab his cock in one hand and fed it into her mouth.

As the American sucked gently on his balls, running her tongue over them too, Amanda jammed his cock right down into her throat, feeling his glans swelling against it. Almost before the heat and wetness of her mouth enclosed him completely he was coming, his cock jerking, and his spunk spattering out, big hot spurts of it. There was so much of it she could not swallow it all and some escaped from the side of her mouth.

The American saw it. She released his balls and moved her lips to Amanda's chin, hoovering up the white liquid, then moving higher still and kissing Amanda full on the lips, producing a tremor in her body that clenched her sex around the fingers that were still inside her.

Chapter Nine

'Morning, darling. Do you want orange?'

Greg was wearing his cotton robe, white with black polka dots. There were distinct bags under his eyes and he hadn't shaved.

'Yes. But nothing to eat. Just coffee.'

He sat at the kitchen table. Amanda had set out the Sunday newspaper, but he didn't even glance at it.

'How are you feeling?' she asked him, setting down a glass of orange juice in front of him.

'Rough.'

'Oh dear.' She stooped and kissed his cheek. He hadn't shaved and the bristles of his beard stung her soft skin. 'Can't take the pace anymore.'

'I thought I took the pace rather well,' he said.

'You did. Very well. In fact you were magnificent.'

Greg did not respond. He drunk the orange juice down in one gulp then sat looking out of the window.

Amanda knew she had to be careful. The party had been a success as far as she was concerned. Not only had she had the most marvellous sex with her husband for the first time in years, no one had said anything that had made him in the least suspicious. It appeared he was convinced by her story that she had no idea it was going to be that sort of party. In the taxi home she had told him she would call Natasha and find out if she too was as surprised as they had been.

'So,' Greg said, 'what are we going to do?'

'Do? About what?'

She put the coffee pot on the table and sat down.

'About last night.'

'What do you mean?'

'Are we going to pretend it never happened?'

'Why? You enjoyed yourself. I enjoyed myself. Is there anything wrong with that?'

'It was an orgy.'

'That's just a word. All I saw was a lot of people having a really good time. No one got hurt did they?'

'I suppose not.'

'You never used to be so conventional.'

'What does that mean?'

'When we first met you were very imaginative.'

'We didn't do it with another girl.'

'So now we have. And you know it was great for both of us. Isn't that all that matters?'

'You let her kiss you.'

'In the heat of the moment. I was very turned on.' She hoped that sounded plausible. This was definitely not the moment to confess to the truth.

'I never found out her name.'

'Whose name?'

'The blonde.'

'She was gorgeous.'

'You were really into it, weren't you?'

'So were you. Don't tell me you didn't have the best sex you've had for years.'

'I did.'

'Don't all men have fantasies about having two women at the same time?'

'I've been too busy with work to have fantasies recently.'

'Well, that's a bad thing, isn't it?'

'Do you want to ring Josef and ask him to invite us next time round?'

'Is that what you want?'

'I don't know, Mandy, I really don't know. It just doesn't feel right.'

He drank his coffee and sat staring out of the window. Amanda thought it wise to leave it at that, to let him work out for himself what he really wanted. She hoped that sexual excitement would overcome his moral qualms.

'It was terribly difficult. She kissed me but fortunately that was all. If she'd gone any further I don't know what I'd have done. I was itching to get at her. I don't think I'd have been able to resist, then the whole thing would have been blown. He was suspicious enough as it was.'

'So what are you going to do now?'

They were sitting in Maggie's front room with large gin and tonics. It had been a beautiful day, the sun warm and the air full of the scent of spring, and she had opened the French windows at the back allowing a pleasant breeze to waft through the house. The sun was so low in the sky, its light was shining horizontally into the West-facing aspect.

Greg had settled down in front of the television. Maggie, anxious for the latest news, had spotted Amanda pottering about in the garden and had invited her in.

'Softly-softly-catchee-monkey,' Amanda said.

'You think he'll go again?'

'He might.'

'Well at least you had a good time. Do you want another gin?'

'Why not? It's such a beautiful day, isn't it?' Amanda was looking out on the garden, the slanting sunlight throwing deep shadows on Maggie's lawn.

Maggie got up to get more ice. She returned with an ice bucket and tongs, then distributed ice cubes between their glasses and mixed fresh drinks. Instead of returning to the armchair she had been sitting on, she handed Amanda her glass then knelt on the sofa beside her.

'Cheers,' she said, clinking their glasses together. 'Here's to new adventures.' She sipped the drink, reached back to put it on the coffee table then put her hand rather self-consciously on Amanda's knee. 'Have you been thinking about me?' she asked, looking straight into Amanda's eyes, her expression suddenly grave.

'Yes.'

'And?'

Why Maggie had suddenly decided she didn't need anonymity anymore and was prepared to come out into the open about her desire, Amanda did not know. But it was quite obvious from the look in her eyes that she had.

Amanda looked at her friend's body. She was wearing a white blouse and a pair of black slacks. Amanda could see her bra under the blouse, a practical style that struggled to contain her large breasts. Boldly, she raised her head and kissed Maggie on the lips very lightly.

'It's too close,' she said.

'Close?'

'I see you practically every day. It might be embarrassing.'

'Not for me.' Maggie's hand climbed Amanda's leg. She was wearing a pair of denim shorts and her legs were bare. 'I've been thinking a lot about you. About what it would be like to take you to my bed. I've got myself into quite a state about it.'

Remembering what it was like was more accurate, Amanda thought, but did not say.

Amanda was concerned. What had happened between them at Adrian's and Natasha's had already changed their relationship even though Maggie didn't know it. She might have been prepared to take it further, to admit to Maggie that she knew the truth and suggest they go to bed together openly, but the events of last night had changed her attitude. She had set out on her sexual odyssey because her sex life at home was virtually non-existent. She had done it because she didn't want to get into an affair that might break up her marriage. Now it seemed possible that Greg's interest in sex could be revived and she could have the best of both worlds, her marriage *and* great sex.

She wanted women sexually, of course. But her desire for lesbian sex, and memories of Monica, were largely a product of sexual dysfunction in her marriage. During the years when Greg had been sexually active it had never occurred to her once to think about Monica, or any other woman. Besides there was always a possibility she might be able to persuade him that it would be a good idea to share a woman between them.

She put her hand on Maggie's to arrest its progress.

'No,' she said firmly. 'I'd love to Maggie, I really would, but it would change everything between us.'

'It might change it for the better.'

'No.' But there was a weakness in her voice and when Maggie pushed against her hand it offered no resistance, Maggie's fingers sliding up to the legs of the shorts and burrowing in underneath them.

'So soft,' she said, as she hooked a finger under the leg of the nylon panties Amanda's was wearing and wriggled down between her labia.

'No,' Amanda said. But this time she clearly meant the opposite. The gin had gone to her head. She felt enveloped in a delicious sense of well being. Her intellectual concerns seemed irrelevant, her bodily needs more important. Did it matter, just this once? She found herself resting her head against the back of the sofa and extending her legs and opening them slightly as she pushed her sex up towards her friend.

Maggie took advantage of her loucheness. She slipped a finger deep into Amanda's vagina. Amanda moaned.

'Isn't that nice?' Maggie asked. She used her other hand to unbutton the denim blouse her friend was wearing, then dipped her head to suck on her breast.

'We shouldn't be doing this,' Amanda said.

'That's what makes it so exciting,' Maggie replied.

Her hand found the zip of the shorts and drew it down.

She pulled her finger out of Amanda's sex. 'I want to kiss it,' she said, with no need to elaborate what 'it' was.

Amanda raised her hips and allowed Maggie to pull the shorts and panties down her legs. Immediately she had stripped them from her ankles she knelt on the floor between Amanda's legs.

'What a beautiful pussy,' she said, staring at the object of her desire.

'You've seen it before, haven't you?'

'What do you mean?' Maggie said with feigned innocence.

'I know the truth, Maggie. It was your scent that gave you away.'

'Are you cross? It was Natasha's idea.'

'It was wonderful. I enjoyed every minute of it. You know that.'

'You're not angry?'

'No.'

'I couldn't go on pretending. That's why I decided I had to come out in the open.'

'Kiss me, then,' Amanda said, her body entirely in control now, her response to Maggie's unequivocal desire making heart thump against her ribs. Somewhere a little voice told her she should not be doing this, but it was easy to ignore.

'Like this,' Maggie said, bending forward. She kissed Amanda's belly, then moved her lips lower pressing her face down between Amanda's thighs.

Amanda felt the hot, wet tongue darting into her labia. She moaned. It was a sensation she didn't think she would ever get over. Men had performed cunnilingus many times, but there was something about a woman's mouth that was so different. It was probably more to do with her mind than her body, the idea that it was a woman, which was taboo, giving the physical sensations an added piquancy.

Maggie's touch was perfect. Her tongue sought out Amanda's clit, first pushing it up as if trying to get underneath it, then dragging it from side to side. She insinuated her hand up between Amanda's thighs and pushed her bunched up fingers into her vagina. It was hot and wet. Slowly, three fingers invaded the tight tube.

'Oh, God, what are you doing to me?' Amanda sighed. Though all this had been completely unexpected, her body's response was instant. She felt the tell-tale signs of orgasm tingling through her nerves, her pulse racing, her nerves alight, her nipples screwing themselves up into tight, hard buds.

She loved sex. She loved it. Every experience she had had in the last few weeks was fresh and vivid in her mind. Images crowded in, each adding to her excitement. She saw Greg lying on top of the blonde, his buttocks driving him forward. She saw Adrian's cock spattering spunk over her face and down on to his black rubber-swathed body. She saw Annie kneeling between her thighs. And now it was Maggie.

Her orgasm was close. 'You're making me come,' she hissed.

'Mmmm . . .' Maggie muttered without breaking her rhythm. Her tongue was insistent, each movement producing a wave of feeling, each wave stretching Amanda further, bringing her orgasm closer. She arched herself off the sofa, allowing Maggie's fingers to penetrate further.

'Mandy! Mandy! Are you here?' It was Greg's voice. It was coming from the garden.

Maggie's tongue did not waiver. She could feel the tension in her friend's body and seemed to determined to relieve it.

'Mandy!' The voice was getting closer.

Amanda felt her whole body clench. Her orgasm peaked. She groaned, her thighs clasped tightly around Maggie's cheeks, her sex contracting around her fingers.

'Mandy! Are you in there?'

As Amanda opened her eyes she saw her husband climbing over the fence that separated their two gardens. He had done it before, coming to get his wife so she could cook him supper.

'Christ,' Amanda said, sitting up.

'Does it matter?' Maggie said lazily, rocking back on her haunches. She pulled her fingers from Amanda's sex then sucked them into her mouth. 'Mmmm . . . nice.'

'For Christ's sake!' Amanda grabbed her shorts and ran into the hall just as Greg got to the French windows. She tried to close the door but the door handle would not latch and she could only leave it ajar.

'Maggie?'

'Hi, Greg, we were just talking about you.'

'Really? Can I come in?'

'You can do anything you like, you know that.' Maggie's voice was low and soft. Her sexual arousal was not going to go away that easily. 'Do you want a drink?'

'No thanks. I thought Mandy might be here.'

'She was. Come over here,' she said.

'What are you doing on your knees?'

Amanda pulled on her shorts and did up her blouse. It was only then she realised she had forgotten her panties. She looked through the gap in the door and saw them by Maggie's knee.

'Now that would be telling wouldn't it?'

'Something to do with these?' Greg said. He stooped and picked up the nylon panties.

'Some things are secret.'

'Perhaps I will have that drink.' He sat on the sofa.

'Help yourself,' Maggie said, sitting down on the sofa next to him.

Amanda saw Greg lean forward and pour himself a gin. She realised she couldn't slip out of the front door and into her house. She didn't have the front door keys. She was trapped. The only way back was through the garden.

'Cheers,' he said, raising his glass. 'So where is my wife?'

'Don't know. She had a drink then said she was going to do some shopping.'

That made it worse, Amanda thought. She couldn't breeze back into the room now pretending to have been to the loo.

'Of course.'

'I've always really fancied you.'

Amanda almost choked. What was Maggie playing at?

'That's a strange coincidence because I've always thought you were gorgeous,' he said. 'Not that I've ever cheated on my wife.'

'Of course not.' Amanda saw Maggie's arm touch Greg's. 'Until last night. But that's not really cheating, is it?' Amanda groaned inwardly. The bitch. She expected Greg to explode, furious she had discussed the subject with Maggie. But his reaction was quite different.

'She told you about that?' he asked quietly.

'We've been friends for a very long time. You know what women are like. The trouble was it made me feel . . .' she wriggled her body against his, 'horny.'

'Really?'

'Yes. Imagining you fucking this beautiful blonde while Mandy looked on. Must have been one hell of a turn on.'

'It was.'

'Certainly turned me on just thinking about it. That's what I was doing. I mean as soon as Mandy had gone I just couldn't stop myself. You found the evidence,' she said, nodding towards the panties he'd dropped on the coffee table. 'I was imagining you doing it to me, with Mandy watching us. That would be fun, wouldn't it?'

'Pity she's not here,' he said.

Amanda watched Maggie's hand snake into his lap. 'Does that matter?'

'I've never cheated on her,' Greg said.

'It wouldn't be cheating. You could tell her. She wouldn't mind. She didn't mind last night did she?'

'No.'

'Well then? Do you know how hot I am, Greg? I mean really hot. My cunt's like molten lava. Did that girl last night have a hot cunt? Did both of them? Must have been a real turn on going from one to the other.'

'God, yes.'

Maggie's hand fastened on his cock. Amanda could see her clasping her fingers around it. There was already a distinct bulge in his trousers. It was quite clear what Maggie had in mind. She had often told Amanda how much she fancied Greg and was obviously going to use this opportunity to fulfil her fantasies. And Amanda could hardly complain. What was sauce for the goose . . . After all she had encouraged her husband to make love to another woman last night, while she watched, so she could hardly object if he did exactly the same thing to her best friend.

'You're very hard already,' Maggie said.

'Look, perhaps this isn't such a good idea,' he said without much conviction.

'OK, well you'd better go home, then.' Confident that he was not going anywhere, Maggie unzipped the fly of his trousers. She delved inside and extracted his cock. 'But why don't you leave this here for me to play with?'

She dropped her mouth onto his erection. He moaned. Amanda saw her lips pursing around his glans, working in and out between them. She sunk her mouth down until his cock disappeared entirely, then pulled her head back, her tongue licking at the sword of flesh.

'Love it,' she said, before plunging down again, this time taking up a regular rhythm.

The expression on Greg's face was a mixture of shock and delight. He had obviously not expected this and looked as though he wasn't sure whether to just lie back and enjoy it or make some effort to stop her. He groaned as she increased the pace, her head rising and falling so fast it was almost a blur.

'No,' he said forcefully. He grabbed her head and pulled her off him.

'Let me,' Maggie said. 'I want it.'

'I want this,' he said. He struggled up from the sofa and pulled Maggie to her feet. Wrapping his arms around her he kissed her full on the mouth. Amanda could see their tongues vying for position as their lips squirmed against each other. A sharp pang of pleasure emanated from her clit, reviving the orgasm she had experienced. It was followed by little twinges of sensation that made her body squirm. She found herself rubbing her arm across her breasts.

Greg's hand had found the zip of Maggie's slacks. Pulling it down he grasped the waistband of the trousers and began pulling them down over her legs. He broke the kiss and dropped to his knees, tugging the slacks down with him.

'My turn now,' he said, grinning up at her.

Maggie raised each leg in turn as he stripped the trousers away. She was wearing bright red French knickers, their hem flounced up giving a good view of the crease of her buttocks where it folded into the top of her thigh. The crotch was loose fitting and Greg had no difficulty in shunting it aside as his tongue delved into her labia, his fingers finding their way under the legs of the knickers at the back. He appeared to have forgotten about the black panties she also claimed to have been wearing.

'Oh Greg . . . Greg . . .' Maggie moaned. He had clearly found his target. Amanda could see Maggie's body shudder. The fingers of Greg's right hand worked down between the cleft of her buttocks. He pushed them upward and two sunk into Maggie's clearly well lubricated Vagina, causing her to moan loudly.

Amanda remembered when he used to do this to her. Sometimes when he got home from work she would come to greet him in the hall, and he'd take her there and then, sinking to his knees and pulling off her clothes. He had a special technique, his artful tongue capable of bringing her off in a matter of seconds. She wondered if he was going to use it now.

He was. His knees began to slide between Maggie's feet, pushing them apart. Slowly, without taking his mouth from her labia, he forced himself between her legs like a limbo dancer until they were spread wide apart and most of his body was on the other side. In this position his head was bent back and his face was horizontal, fitting perfectly against her sex. Extracting his fingers from her vagina, he held the gusset of the red knickers aside with his hand while his tongue licked the whole crease of her sex, from one end to the other.

This had always driven Amanda wild. It clearly had the same effect on Maggie. She was bending her legs at the knee, as if sitting on his face, opening herself wider for him. The expression of ecstasy on her face was obvious, her mouth open and her eyes tightly closed. His tongue ploughed the long furrow, teasing her clitoris at one end and burrowing into the hole of her anus at the other, the long journey in between producing a whole panoply of glorious sensation.

'Greg, Greg,' Maggie cried.

This spectacle was creating a huge wave of pleasure in Amanda too. She was rubbing her hand between her legs, but needed more. She wriggled the fingers of one hand past the leg of the shorts and into her vagina, while the other hand rubbed the material against her clit.

She knew what Greg would do next. She saw his hand groping at the back of the knickers, until he could get hold of the gusset. As he felt Maggie's body beginning to lurch towards climax he gathered the material in his fist so it bunched into a thick string, he pulled his mouth away and tugged the knickers backward sharply. The string of nylon had been resting at one side of her labia. Suddenly it was forced down between them, impacting on her clit like a hammer blow.

Maggie literally screamed. It was exactly what she needed, the long strokes of his tongue taking her to the brink and this sudden, almost brutal, treatment taking her over it. Her body quivered violently. The explosion of feeling knocked her off balance and she stumbled back, to prevent herself from falling.

'Christ, what have you done to me?' she said looking down at him.

'Take your blouse off,' he said, clearly not finished with her, 'and your knickers.'

Maggie stared into his eyes as she unbuttoned the blouse, the look of lust she saw there exciting her as much as anything else had. The clasp of her bra was at the front. She freed it and let her breasts loose. They trembled at their freedom, their nipples like oddly elongated rosehips. She skinned the now damp knickers down over her thighs and let them fall to the floor, kicking them away from her with her foot. Her pubes were sparsely covered with black hair, most of it already wet and plastered back against her body.

'What do you want?' she said, though it was quite obvious. She looked up towards the door and caught a glimpse of Amanda, trying to tell her with her eyes that there was no reason for her not to join in.

But there was. There was every reason. If she walked in on them now she would have to express a shock and horror she did not feel. She was not jealous. After what she had done that would be hypocritical, particularly after last night. If she just breezed in, pulled her clothes off and joined them, without batting an eye, Greg was bound to be suspicious. Even after last night that was hardly a natural reaction to finding your best friend and neighbour having it off with your husband. He was bound to be suspicious and that was the last thing she wanted. Having got him this far, Amanda didn't want to go back to square one.

Greg got up and stripped off his clothes. His cock was throbbing visibly. He took hold of Maggie and manoeuvred her around until she was kneeling on the edge of the sofa, her buttocks tilted up towards him, her big breasts hanging down in fleshy inverted pyramids. He came up behind her and poked his cock between her legs.

'I used to have dreams about you doing this to me,' Maggie said, not caring if Amanda heard. She'd said as much to her face.

'Like this?' He bucked his hips. His cock sunk into her. She was tight and very wet.

'Yes, God, yes. That's wonderful. Christ, Greg . . .'

Amanda's sex had reacted almost as strongly as Maggie's. She felt it flex around her fingers. Her clitoris was alive, throbbing violently as she shunted it from side to side.

Greg's fingers clawed at Maggie's hips, pulling her back on him as he powered forward, his legs bent slightly at the knee. He began to hammer into her with a relentless motion, pulling almost all the way out before plunging all the way in again.

Amanda could not see his cock but she could see his balls jiggling between his legs, and Maggie's breasts swaying with each impact, and hear the loud thwack their flesh made as his belly slapped against the meaty curves of her buttocks.

'No, no,' Maggie said breathlessly, turning to look at him over her shoulder, her eyes flaring with excitement.

'What then?' he said, stopping his thrusts.

'Bugger me, Greg. Please,' she said.

Amanda had to suppress a gasp. The words made her sex spasm again, her sphincter contracting. The hard cock that had penetrated her rear so recently had left an impression that this suggestion revived, her whole anus suddenly tingling.

Greg did not hesitate. He pulled out of her cunt and took his erection in his hand, pressing against his new target. It was wet enough to provide all the lubrication he needed. He edged forward, the little ring of muscles providing an initial resistance. With a second shove, he broke the barrier but only penetrated as far as the ridge of his glans.

Maggie let out a scream. It was the sound of pain laced with electrifying pleasure.

Greg pushed again. This time he plunged right into her, all resistance gone, his cock lancing up into her hot, tight anus.

Another scream, with the same mélange of pain and pleasure.

Greg pulled back, then drove forward again just as forcibly as he'd done in her cunt, his buttocks dimpling with the effort. He ran his left hand over her back and down onto her breast, searching for her nipple. When he found it he pinched it between his thumb and forefinger and dragged her breast out by it, stretching the flesh like elastic. At the same time his other hand slid down between her legs. His finger tweaked her clitoris briefly, then probed lower into the crease of her labia. The mouth of her vagina was closed by the breadth of his cock in her other passage but he wriggled one finger then two into it, then pushed them up into the velvety wet interior.

'Oh, God,' Maggie cried loudly. She was moaning continuously now, each forward thrust of his cock producing a cry, each cry louder and more keening.

Amanda was glad. It masked her own gasps of pleasure as her fingers pistoned into her sex and she pummelled at her clit. Her orgasm was approaching as rapidly as Maggie's.

Suddenly Maggie's body reared up from the sofa until her back was almost touching Greg's chest, then fell forward again, shuddering, her body rigid. Amanda could not watch any more. She leant against the hall wall for support and closed her eyes, needing to concentrate on her own internal feelings, her climax spreading through her like waves of heat, demanding all her attention.

When she opened her eyes Greg's hands were planted firmly on Maggie's hips again and Maggie was silent.

He pulled out of her.

Daring to poke her head round the door to get a better view, Amanda saw the tip of Greg's cock. He had pressed himself into the soft flesh of Maggie's buttocks just as the man at the party had done. His right hand came up and he rubbed the ridge of his glans with his fingers. It was the most sensitive part of his body, Amanda knew. She saw his cock recoil, then swell. He moaned and wrapped his fist around the tender flesh just as an arc of spunk jetted out of him, landing in big white gobs all down Maggie's back and over her buttocks. He milked it slowly, determined to extract every last drop.

'Hi, Amanda.'

Amanda recognised the voice. It was Natasha. 'Hello.'

'I thought it would be better to wait until he'd gone to

work before I called you,' she said. It was Monday morning and Greg had left for work an hour ago.

'Thanks, it would have been awkward.'

'So, did you have a good time?'

'Great. I can't tell you. I never knew such things went on.'

'And did lover boy behave himself?'

'Only in all the wrong ways. He was as turned on as I was, fortunately. It seems to have had an amazing effect on his libido.' She was thinking about yesterday.

'That's what you had in mind, wasn't it?'

'Exactly. What happened to you and Adrian by the way? I was looking for you.'

'We had to give a command performance.'

'What does that mean?'

'Josef. He likes to watch. You'd gone off with one of his bimbos apparently, so he needed a replacement. He chose me. Very flattering really, considering he could have had any one at the party. And there were some gorgeous women, weren't there?'

'Absolutely.'

'I had to do this number with the blonde while he watched. He's into seeing women doing it with dildoes. In the end he gave me this strap-on version. It's got this little finger on the inside. Just sort of curls into you. While I was pushing the big end into her, this one on the inside was working against my clitty. God, it was great. I've got to order one for myself. Never seen it before.'

'And Ade?'

'Oh, he stayed downstairs in the main room. He likes that. Apparently this big brunette took a fancy to him and she had a friend. She wanted to be spanked. Are you into that? I'm not. Course, everyone wanted to watch that, so he bent her over this stool and laid into her with his hand. Then of course she was really hot and wanted to be fucked. So she got down on top of him on the carpet and her friend whipped her with a crop while he gave her everything he'd got. Quite a show by all accounts.'

'Sounds like fun.'

'Anyway, do you think lover boy is up to a second round?'

'Another party?'

'Unless you'd like to bring him here? You know you're welcome anytime. I have to say, he was a bit of a hunk. I wouldn't mind having him strapped up in the room, nice and helpless. There are several things I'd like to do to him . . .'

'I don't think he's ready for that yet.'

'Pity. Still, one day. Anyway, there is another party if you fancy it. Different this time.'

'Different?'

'It's a black room party.'

'What does that mean?'

'Well, firstly it's not just for couples. There're singles too. Single women, that is. Which means there're more women than men and naturally all the women have to swing both ways.'

'Why naturally?' Amanda didn't understand.

'You'll see. It's better if it's all a surprise. Do you think Greg will go?'

'After yesterday I'm sure of it.'

'What happened yesterday?'

'He got rather involved with Maggie.'

'Really?' Natasha didn't sound all that surprised. 'And?'

'I think he's rediscovered the fact that sex can be fun. Ironic, I suppose. Maggie's fancied him for years. I don't know why I just didn't get her to seduce him in the first place. We could have shared him between us.'

'Maggie's not into sharing,' Natasha said quietly.

'What? I thought she came around to you and Adrian?'

'That's not what I meant.'

'So what did you mean?'

'It's just she can get very carried away. She's into sex. She loves it. But she sometimes confuses lust and love. There was

189

a time when she was getting very funny about Adrian. Getting jealous about me, for God's sake. I think she wanted to run off with him. Adrian had to put her straight.'

'I didn't know.'

'There's no reason why you should. But she doesn't come around to see us as often as she used to, and that's the reason.'

'Will she be at this party?'

'Doubt it.'

'No problem, then. Give me the address.'

Natasha gave her the details and Amanda wrote them down.

'And when?'

'Next Saturday at eight,' Natasha said.

'See you there. Can't wait.'

And that was true.

Chapter Ten

'Are you ready?' he shouted up the stairs.

'Just two minutes. Call the taxi. I'll be down.'

Amanda pulled the second stocking taut and clipped it into her black suspender, then adjusted the tension so the welt of the stocking was pulled into a peak on her thigh. The suspender belt was black lace, the suspenders made from satin. She had debated whether she should wear panties and had decided there was something extremely sexy about sliding them sinuously inch by inch down her long legs. She would turn her back and pout her bottom as she did it, revealing her sex to the eyes of a stranger for the first time, her labia pursed between the cheeks of her bottom. The thought made her pulse race.

She had been right about Greg. He had jumped at the chance. The hesitancy he had displayed on Sunday morning had vanished. As soon as she mentioned another party he had told her, unequivocally, that they should go. It was, he told her, an opportunity to rekindle the flames of their sex life. He said it as if it was all his idea.

So far, however, the fire might have been laid with dry kindling, but in the week since his encounter with Maggie it had not been lit. Perhaps that was not a fair test Amanda decided. Greg had been working late almost every night. He hadn't got home till eleven and on Wednesday he didn't come home till one.

Amanda had thought of jogging his interest with a black basque and sheer stockings, and the ankle boots he loved, but didn't want to be disappointed by a plea of tiredness so decided to wait until an evening when he had not been working so hard. She could wait. When he announced he was going to be home early she would greet him at the door in the ankle boots and perhaps nothing else and see what effect that had on his hopefully rekindled passion.

She had not seen Maggie all week either. They'd spoken briefly on the phone on Monday afternoon, when she'd told her about Natasha's invitation, but since then she had heard nothing. Like Greg she appeared to be working late, even later than him in fact, each night Amanda hearing her arrive home some time after him.

She had not mentioned Maggie to him and he hadn't mentioned her. She was definitely going to tell him she knew what had happened but would probably not reveal the circumstances. She planned on telling him that Maggie had spilt the beans and that she didn't mind in the least but she thought she'd wait to see what happened after his second party. Perhaps, after what Maggie had done to her, there might be an occasion when they invited themselves next door and both enjoyed Maggie's hospitality. Now, she thought, that would be something to look forward to.

'Come on,' Greg shouted again.

Quickly she hooked the black panties around her ankles and drew them up over the stockings. They were a stunning design, the black satin no more than a wide V of material that followed the line of her pelvis up to her hips. A similar chevron cut diagonally across her buttocks. She was not wearing a bra.

She had chosen a shiny cream dress with a round neck and no sleeves, the skirt just low enough to cover the tops of the stockings. She stepped into it and zipped it up before climbing into her shoes, which were a white patent leather and extremely high-heeled, shoes she had only ever worn before in the bedroom, the shoes of a whore.

Cautiously, the shoes making her take small steps, she walked downstairs.

'Hey, you look great,' Greg said, which was an improvement in itself she thought. He had barely mentioned her appearance in the last years.

'Thank you. And this?' She pulled the hem of the dress up until he could see her stockings.

'Even better.'

'I'm sorry you've been so busy this week,' she said. 'I was planning on getting all dressed up for you.'

'That would have been nice.'

'But I thought you'd be too tired.'

'You were right. Next week things should have calmed down.' He didn't sound very convincing on that score.

'I hope so. I really enjoyed myself last week. It was great to have the old Greg back. You're very fanciable you know. And you haven't lost your touch.'

'Here's the taxi,' he said, glancing out of the window. He seemed glad to change the subject.

The journey to Edington Road in Fulham took thirty minutes. Amanda felt her own excitement increasing. She hoped that all this would bring Greg back into her life sexually, but separate from that there was the mystery that Natasha had hinted at. What surprises was this evening going to bring?

The taxi pulled up outside a rather nondescript house. Though it was obviously large, the white stucco exterior badly needed replacing. There were two plastic dustbins at the front where there had once been a gate, and the small front garden was overgrown, the litter that had blown in from the street collecting in one corner. There were three stone steps up to the front door, all of which were cracked and chipped and the door itself had seen better days, the green paint flaking and one of its two long, thin frosted glass panels badly cracked. As the house was double fronted, there were large bay windows on either side of the front door but thick curtains had been drawn over both of them.

'Not Bishop's Avenue,' Greg said, ringing the bell. They could hear the drone of music and voices from inside.

'Welcome.' The door had been opened my a redhead. Despite the fact she was wearing shoes with a heel quite as high as the ones Amanda wore she was still no more than five feet tall. She was dressed in a lace catsuit, the material flattening her firm breasts back against her chest, and revealing the fact that she was not wearing panties. Her pubic hair was short and stubbly.

'Greg and Amanda,' Greg said.

'Friends of Natasha, right?'

'Right.'

'Come in. Follow me,' she said, closing the door then turning tail and walking down a long dingy hallway. She had a tight, pert bottom, and her short legs were shapely, the high heels firming their muscles.

She opened a door on the right hand side and ushered them through. The room beyond was large, once the sitting room and dining room of the substantial Victorian house. It contained about thirty people. Where in Bishop's Avenue the couples had all been smartly dressed in evening clothes, here the fetishistic designs predominated. There were women in beautifully cut *haute couture* but most wore more exotic outfits. There were dresses in tight rubber, with holes cut in the material to reveal breasts and buttocks, there were leather catsuits and incredibly tight leather shorts, and women who wore clinging strapless tube dresses covered in sequins. A tall brunette wore thigh boots and an arrangement of leather straps, extending down from a studded collar around her neck, the straps arranged around her breasts, squeezing them out slightly, then down in a V to her navel where they were attached to a metal ring just above her pubis. From this another strap wound around her hips and two very thin ones snaked between her legs, clinging to the flesh on either side of her labia and leaving her sex itself exposed.

The men were just as diverse. But though some, like Greg, had opted for a suit, there were others who had been more daring, some in transparent nylon briefs, others in leather chaps, like cowboys wore, but with nothing underneath, and some in tiny leather thongs that struggled to contain their genitals.

'Drinks are over there,' the redhead said. 'I'm Cherry, by the way.' She took a small loop of blue silk and touched it against Amanda's dress. It was backed with Vélcro and stuck to the material. She applied a red loop to Greg's jacket then turned and looked up at him, having to tilt her head right back. 'I hope I'll see you later.' She turned and went back towards the hall as the doorbell rang again.

Amanda noticed all the men were wearing the loops, some blue and some red, but not all the women.

There was every sort of booze except champagne but no one to appeared to be serving it, so Greg poured himself a scotch and mixed his wife a gin and tonic.

'Your first time?' The man standing next to Amanda asked. He wore a thong in a leopard skin print and a short halter top but his body was soft, and though not fat, had little muscle tone.

'Yes.'

'Yes,' Greg added, handing Amanda her drink. 'How did you guess?'

'The clothes. First timers usually come fully dressed. But it's better to wear something distinctive.'

'Better?' Amanda queried.

'In the black room. You'll see.'

'What's the black room?' Greg asked.

Amanda had not passed on all that Natasha said, fearing that he might use it as an excuse not to go.

'You *are* new,' the man said. He touched his finger against the side of his nose. 'You'll see.'

The redhead brought two women into the room. One was wearing an incredibly tight red patent leather basque, its cups tucked under her large breasts. The red stockings clipped into the basque's suspenders had black seams. The other woman wore a catsuit in the same material over which was a tight waspie laced up at the front. The ends of the laces dangled down between her legs. She wore ankle boots very similar to the pair Amanda had, their heels tipping her feet almost vertical.

'Ladies and gentlemen.'

At first they could not see where the female voice came from. Then a woman stepped on to a small stool at one end of the room, her head and shoulders raised above the crowd. She had long black hair which had been permed out into frizzy strands and very heavy make-up, her lips a dark red, her dark brown eyes highlighted with dark eyeshadow. She was staring around the room, looking at the guests one by one.

'Ladies and gentlemen, thank you for coming.'

The hall door opened and Amanda saw Natasha and Adrian slip in. Natasha was wearing a black silk slip with spaghetti straps and lacy hold up stockings. Adrian was stripped to the waist and wore leather trousers. She wished Natasha had given her more clue about the dress code, though she supposed she wouldn't have been able to do much about it for fear of frightening Greg off.

Not that on the current evidence she need have worried on that score. She glanced down and saw a large bulge distending the front of his trousers. He, in turn, was looking at the woman immediately in front of him, the rubber shorts she was wearing cut so high and tight that the legs were biting into her buttocks. The crotch had buried itself deep between her legs.

'As always there're some new faces and some familiar faces, so for those of you who have not been before I'll explain the rules. Cherry has divided all the couples into red and blue. In the hall outside you will find a red door and blue door. When we begin the couples will go through the appropriate door. We will then divide the single women up equally and send them in after you. You will then select your partners. As there are more women than men some women will find themselves with a female partner. As always, once you have found your partner you must sit down. You can only select from people who are standing. Is that clear?'

There was a chorus of assent. A couple of men shouted that they wanted to get on with it.

'Right, so if you'd line up. Reds first.'

The woman got off the stool and strode towards the hall door as people began to group together, their red loops of material checked by Cherry who then marched them out into the hall.

Curiously Amanda found this all very unerotic. Whereas Bishop's Avenue had been glamorous and immensely exciting, there was something rather sordid and practical about this routine. That didn't mean she had any intention of leaving. There were several men who she would be happy to select and judging by the voluptuous women she was sure Greg would feel the same.

Greg smiled back at her as he joined the queue of 'reds'. He was the last through the door.

The 'blues' began to bunch together. Amanda could see the woman who had addressed them more clearly now. She was wearing a black velvet cloak with white silk lining. Underneath Amanda caught glimpses of a short, orange dress.

With the other men and women Amanda filed past Cherry, who checked she was wearing the right ribbon. They all walked down the hall to a brightly painted blue door. Inside was a square room with a number of straight-backed wooden chairs that looked as though they had come from a job lot at an auction. There was a large window at one end which was covered with heavy black drapes and similar curtaining covering the whole of one wall.

The 'blues' stood about, smiling at each other, and eyeing each other with obvious interest, as four or five women without ribbons walked into the room.

Amanda saw Cherry close the door and heard a key rattle in a lock. Immediately all the lights went out and the room was plunged into total and absolute blackness. The black room, Amanda, thought at once, this is what it meant.

In a second she felt a hand groping her breast. It squeezed it hard, as if trying to guess its weight then left, obviously not satisfied. A second hand stroked her thigh, moving up under her dress until it was tweaking the suspender that held her stocking. Another hand pulled her forward and she felt a man's mouth closing on her lips. The latter did not belong to the former. The hand on her thighs was jerked away, only to be replaced immediately by another, this one on her buttocks. The kiss was broken. She sensed the man's head being pulled away.

The room was totally black. After a few minutes in a dark room the eyes usually adjust and light can be seen coming from little gapes under the doors and windows, but in this room there wasn't a hint of light anywhere. It was like being blind.

She remembered what the man outside had said. Wearing something distinctive made it easier to be recognised by touch alone.

Amanda felt fingers forcing their way between her legs. They pushed the crotch of her panties up into her labia. A mouth brushed against hers. It was undoubtedly a woman. Arms wrapped around her back and the woman kissed her full on the lips, her tongue plunging into her mouth. It felt big and wet.

So far Amanda had been too surprised to do anything but be passive. But now she had worked out what was happening she decided to try and get what she wanted. Tonight she was not in the mood for lesbian sex. She wanted a man. One man in particular among the 'blues' had caught her eye. He was tall and blond, with long hair parted on the left, a lock of it falling occasionally into his eyes. He was wearing a white T-shirt and a pair of denim jeans that had been sawn off at the top of his thighs. He was young and muscular. While Greg was next door, probably trying to find the woman in the rubber hot pants, she thought the blond would be ample diversion for her.

But how to find him? That was the problem. He had been standing by the door when the lights went out, but where was the door? Deprived of the sense of sight she had no way of knowing. The woman who had kissed her had turned her round so she had lost any sense of which direction the door was. All she could do was what the others were doing, grope around in the hope she would feel the cotton of a T-shirt or the denim of the improvised shorts.

She stepped forward, her hands out in front of her and bumped into the pneumatic chest of a woman, her hands clawing at bare flesh. As they slipped down she felt a shiny cold material and wondered if it might be the woman in the red patent leather basque. They passed each other without further ado.

Amanda felt a hand touch her leg again. Again it travelled up towards her crotch, groping around the front of her panties. She touched the arm that was attached to it but felt a sleeve. The blond had bare arms. She pushed the hand away and stepped backward into another woman. The woman's hands snaked around her back and down over her belly, one hugging her back until she could feel the woman's breasts being crushed by her shoulder blades while the other pulled up the hem of the dress and tried to lever its way into her panties.

She twisted away. She took two steps forward and collided with a man. He was sideways to her and as she felt his naked arm. It might be her target. But she sensed another body too. Groping to her left she found a woman, her flesh encased in tight leather straps. It was definitely the woman she'd seen in the harness. The man was embracing her tightly. The darkness had magnified her sense of touch but it had done the same for her hearing and sense of smell. She was sure she could hear the unmistakable squelch of penetration and smell the musky aroma of sex. The woman in the leather harness had got her man.

Fortunately it was not the man in the denim shorts. She pushed her hand on to the man's chest and discovered only naked flesh. It was possible, she supposed, the man had stripped off his T-shirt, but she doubted it.

Just as she was moving off, two hands grabbed her by the shoulders and spun her round. A mouth dipped down to hers and she felt a tongue pushing between her lips. As she allowed herself to be kissed, her chest butted against the hardness of another man. She wrapped her arms around him and felt his cock bulging against her belly. The material on his back was thin like cotton. She moved her hand to his arm and found it bare. Quickly she glided her other hand down to his buttocks and was sure the rough material that covered it was denim. She pushed it lower and came across the flesh of his thigh. She'd found him.

'Find a seat,' she said, desperate not to lose him again.

'No,' he whispered in her ear, his hot breath exciting her. 'Follow me.'

He took her hand in his and started to pull her across the room. As he did she felt a woman's body block their path. She caressed Amanda's body briefly then turned her attention to the man but somehow he managed to lever her aside.

They reached the wall and he began edging around it, pressing her back too, so her back was against it and she presented the minimum target to roving hands. He stopped. She heard a swish of material, then the creak of a door being opened. He pulled her forward again. The carpet under her feet was gone and her shoes clacked on a wooden floor. There was another creak as a door closed.

'It's a short cut,' he said, tugging on her hand.

She heard her feet clacking on the floor as they walked three or four yards.

'Close your eyes tight,' he said.

She did as she was told but even then the sudden shock of light burnt through her eyelids and it took several seconds before she dared to open them.

He had opened a door in a short corridor. Immediately in front of them was a flight of stairs.

'Mmm, what a prize,' he said. 'You're even better than I remember you.' He grinned, revealing perfectly white teeth.

'So are you. But weren't we supposed to wait?'

'I have special privileges. This is my sister's house. I'm the only one who knows about that door.'

'That's cheating,' Amanda said.

'Do you care?' He smiled. It was totally disarming. 'Don't tell me you're not turned on.'

He was right. Amanda discovered the mauling from all the unseen hands had left her incredibly aroused. Apart from that she had got the one man in the room she really fancied.

'All's fair in love and war,' she said.

He took her hand and led her up the stairs. There was a long corridor at the top lined with identical doors.

'You choose,' he said. 'They're all unoccupied at the moment.'

She opened the door to her left and walked inside. The room was more smartly decorated than she might have expected from downstairs. The walls were painted a light pink, and there were some still-life prints, mostly with a predominating pink colouring. The bed had a pink counterpane and the windows were curtained with a pattern that featured red poppies.

'We don't have to do anything,' he said, sitting on the edge of the bed.

'I hope you're joking,' Amanda said coming up to him. She took his chin in her hand and tilted his face up towards her. 'I've been imagining what I was going to do to you ever since I set eyes on you.'

'Me too. You're gorgeous. Do you want to tell me your name? It's not obligatory.'

'Mandy.'

'Alan.' He extended his hand and she shook it with an elaborate mime.

'Well that's the pleasantries over.' She felt the same kind of excitement she'd experienced the first time she'd walked into Annie and Phil's house. There was something wonderfully wanton and wicked about being in a room with a total stranger when the only item on the agenda was sex. It aroused her in a way nothing else had. It was freeing. She didn't have to conform to any stereotype of what a woman should or should not do. She was going to be fucked, whatever happened. Similarly the man did not have to pretend. It didn't matter what they did, or how they went about it. It didn't matter if she was outrageous and took the initiative, or let him do it all. The end result was going to be the same.

She reached behind her back and pulled the zip of her dress down.

'Makes such a sexy sound, doesn't it?' he said.

'Come to think of it, it does.' She pushed the shoulder straps off the dress and allowed it to fall to the floor, stepping out of it then stooping to pick it up.

'Gorgeous,' he said, his eyes roaming the black lingerie.

'Now it's your turn.' She pushed him back on to the bed and attacked the fly of the denim. It was fastened with little metal studs. She sprung them open and his cock burst out, already very hard.

'How lovely,' she said, cupping it in her hands and kissing the very tip.

He struggled up and pulled off his T-shirt, then kicked off his shoes and pulled the denim shorts down. He wasn't wearing pants or socks. His body was hairless except for thin blonde hair around his cock.

'So what do we do now, I wonder.'

'What do you usually do?' she said.

'To tell you the truth, I don't often come to Jan's parties.'

'You knew about the secret door. Don't tell me you haven't used it before.'

'I have but, would you believe only once?'

'You certainly know how to grope about in the dark.'

'I know what I like. And I generally find a way to get it.'

'Well, then?'

He caught her by the arm and pulled her down onto the bed, kissing her full on the mouth, his cock nudging into the lace of her suspender belt. She felt her body melt with passion as his arms wrapped around her and hugged her tight.

'Shall I take your panties off?' he asked.

She nodded.

He grabbed the top of her panties and pulled them down to her knees, holding them until she extracted her legs one by one. Then he rolled on top of her and forced his thighs down between hers.

'I think we've had enough foreplay, don't you?' he said, guiding the tip of his cock down into her labia.

'I couldn't agree more.' It was true. Her vagina was liquid, her juices leaking out over his cock. There was something going on here she didn't quite understand. Over the last weeks she had had incredibly strong sexual feelings, her body almost overwhelmed by the things that had been done to it, every orifice penetrated, every erogenous zone primed, pampered and caressed. But none of those feelings could hold a candle to what she was feeling now and she wasn't at all sure why.

Alan rose above her, looking down into her face. His cock sawed up and down in the slit of her sex, its passage oiled by her copious juices. Each time it nosed against her clitoris she felt a shock of pleasure so huge any one of them could have sent her into orgasm.

He arched his body over her and bent his head, sucking on her nipple. In fact he sucked most of her breast into his mouth, spreading his lips around it and using his tongue to flick her nipple from side to side. His mouth felt like a furnace, its heat increasing her own. She moaned loudly. He transferred his attentions to her other breast, doing exactly the same thing. She thought she would come just like this. The treatment was making her clitoris throb violently but her nipples felt just as sensitive.

'What do you want, Mandy?' he said.

203

She didn't understand. She thought it was perfectly obvious what she wanted, every muscle in her body and every nerve trying to express her urgent need.

'You,' she said. 'I've never wanted anyone more in my life.' And that was true. One hundred percent true. She didn't know if it was because of the bizarre way they'd met, whether the extraordinary prologue to their encounter had mashed her nerves into new levels of sensitivity, or whether it was just him, just something about his body and the way he looked at her, and that lock of blond hair falling over his forehead, that was causing it. But it didn't matter. The only thing that mattered was persuading him to put that big hard, throbbing, circumcised cock deep into her body.

He slid his hand up to her mouth, supporting his whole weight above her on one arm, then caressed her lips with one finger. Again for some reason she didn't understand this produced a rush of sensation. Then he replaced his finger with the tip of his tongue, running it along her top lip and over her bottom without venturing inside.

His cock had not stopped gently sawing between her legs, the short journey producing a whole catalogue of different sensations, sharp and tingling as it brushed her clit, warm and sensuous as it nudged against the bottom of her vagina. If he continued to do this, so methodically, she knew she would not be able to stop herself from coming.

'You're making me come,' she murmured.

'I know. I can feel it. Do it for me Mandy. I want to feel it. I love to feel it.'

That was all she needed. If he wanted it that made it all right. She released the few strands of control that had not already broken and felt a huge wave of relief. The relief was immediately joined by a rush of pure pleasure. It was odd to come without any penetration, but as his cock nudged into her clitoris again that's exactly what she did, her sex convulsing, her body locked, the pleasure flooding over her like a tidal wave.

Exactly at that moment he centred his cock on her vagina and thrust into her as smoothly as if it had been rehearsed. He penetrated deep. That was odd too. His cock had not looked particularly large, or so she'd thought, and yet, as it thrust into her, she had never felt so completely and utterly filled. It seemed to stretch her in every direction and that stretching created a whole new set of pleasures.

She thought she heard herself scream. She was coming again. Or perhaps it was just her original orgasm being pushed to new heights. Her sex contracted like a fist, grasping the rod of steel inside it, feeling every last inch.

He didn't move. He didn't try to pound in and out of her but waited until her crisis had passed. Then he slowly pulled out of her, a movement that seemed to go on forever, and pushed back in again.

'Oh, God this is wonderful,' she said.

'That's because you want it so much,' he whispered, the breath from his mouth curling into her ear and producing another tortuous thrill.

He thrust deeper. There was a barrier there, at the top of her body, and he was butting against it. He withdrew again, the long journey down her vagina making her body quiver, the feeling of loss, of emptiness soon replaced by the equal and opposite sensation, of being found and filled completely once again. This time as he battered against her womb she had the feeling that she was opening for him, like the blossoming of a flower, and that he had penetrated beyond her last, secret barrier, where no man had been before.

Of course, that made her come. His glans pulsing in this new place was too much to take. She arched off the bed, every muscle as stretched as the flesh of her cunt, and came with an explosion, like a hundred fireworks, the light behind her tightly shut eyes pulsating sheets of crimson and scarlet.

He wasn't finished with her yet. Suddenly she felt him sliding down the bed, his cock pulling away. Before she could protest his mouth was slipping over her belly and his hands had hooked themselves under her thighs, lifting her buttocks off the bed and presenting her sex to his mouth. It all took less than a fraction of a second. One moment he was inside her, his cock impaled in her, the next his tongue was pressing against her clitoris and once again she was prone to feelings she could hardly believe. His lips circled her clit and began to suck. She felt it being drawn up and out, pulled away until it was elongated and most of it was firmly in his mouth. Having captured it successfully and tenderised it, he moved his mouth from side to side, pulling it this way and that.

She had never felt anything like this. Never. It was wonderful. It was better than wonderful. Sensations rushed through her nerves, her clit producing waves of them, but waves were so close together it was almost impossible to tell the peak of one from the trough of the next. It all blurred together, creating another orgasm which she had to believe was the last. Her body could just not take any more.

But she was wrong.

As he felt her body relax, as the tensions of another orgasm melted away, he lowered her down on to the bed. In an almost balletic movement he thrust himself up on top of her once more, his cock lunging into her vagina without touching her labia at all. This time there was no barrier to break. She had never felt so open, so completely exposed, the very core of her, that she knew now no one had ever touched before, laid bare.

His glans thrust up into the tenderest part of her. Immediately she began to spasm again. She could not control it even if she wanted to and she didn't. She wrapped her arms around his back and clung to him, knowing by some instinct that this time he was going to come too. As her sex clenched around him she felt his glans jerking too, the shaft that supported it trapped by the tight confines of her sex, but his glans free, bursting through into that secret place where it had space to jet its spunk with no restriction.

'Are you all right?' he said when it was over and they had rolled apart.

'What did you do to me?'

'I was going to ask you the same question.'

'It's never been like that for me.'

'Nor me.'

She smiled. 'I bet you say that to all the girls.'

'As a matter of fact I don't,' he said earnestly.

And she believed him.

They didn't wait for a taxi. Though it was late they imagined there would be plenty cruising in the Fulham Road. Besides, Mandy needed the fresh air. She needed it badly.

'So?' Greg asked as they walked down the road. 'Did you have a good time?' He asked the question as if he didn't want to know the answer. That was fortunate because Mandy certainly didn't want to tell him the truth.

'Fine. How about you?'

'Boring,' he said.

Before, Mandy might have thought that answer disappointing, indicating that Greg was keen to slip back to his old ways. But at the moment she just couldn't think of anything but her body. It was weak. Weaker than it had ever been after her sessions with the two couples. So weak she could hardly think straight at all.

They got a black cab almost immediately and Greg gave him the address.

As the cab turned down Edington Road from whence they had come, Greg tried to tell the driver not to go that way. But it was too late. The glass between driver and passenger was jammed and by the time Greg got it open they were half way down the road.

Amanda didn't think it made any difference, but then in her mood nothing did. Nor did it really register with her that as they turned into the next street, Maggie O'Keefe's car was parked on the corner.

Chapter Eleven

The van arrived at ten o'clock. Two men got out and opened the back door. They extracted a large estate agent's sign declaring that Rogers and Rogers were the agents and that a house was for sale. The men marched it over to Maggie's front gate and began hammering it into the ground. When it was secured they got into their van and drove off. It was Monday morning.

'Can I have Maggie O'Keefe, please?'

Amanda had seen the sign going up from her bedroom window. She assumed it was a mistake and that she'd better tell her friend as soon as possible. She sat on the edge of the bed with the phone in her hand.

'Who's calling?'

'Mandy Landseer.'

There was a click on the line then, 'Ms Landseer,' the female voice emphasised the "Ms", 'Ms O'Keefe is away on business.'

'Oh, right. When will she be back?'

'I'm not sure. Can I get her to call you, or can someone else help?'

'It's personal. Just give her a message will you. Say I called.'

'Certainly.' The woman hung up without saying goodbye.

Amanda went to the window and read the estate agent's number off the board, then dialled it.

'Rogers and Rogers.'

'Hello, could I speak to someone about number sixteen, Churchton Road.'

'Hold the line.'

'That was quick.' It was a man's voice.

'Beg your pardon?' Amanda said.

'We've only just put the sign up.'

'That's why I'm ringing. I think there's been a mistake.'

'A mistake? What sort of mistake? Have they put it on the wrong house?'

'Yes, I'm sure they have.'

'What number are you?'

'Eighteen.'

'Oh, Christ, the stupid buggers. All right I'll get them right around. Sorry about that, love. Mistakes happen.'

'No, I mean they've put it up at sixteen.'

'What do you mean?'

'That's the mistake.'

'That's not a mistake. That's right.' His tone changed. 'What are you on about, love?'

'My neighbour's not moving.'

'Really?' His derision was clear. 'Have you told her that? Sorry love, got work to do.'

The dialling tone stung her ear.

She got up and stared at the sign. Maggie was a good friend. A very good friend. Admittedly she hadn't seen her yesterday or for over a week for that matter. In fact Amanda hadn't seen her since she'd watched her being fucked so comprehensively by her husband the Sunday before last, but she was sure that if anything dramatic had happened she would have at least telephoned her. She always had before.

It was only then she remembered that her car had been parked just around the corner from Edginton Road. Had she been at the party? She hadn't seen her if she had and she hadn't made any mention of the fact she was planning to go either.

Amanda went downstairs for her address book. Something was wrong. She felt it instinctively. The trouble was she hadn't the faintest idea what. Perhaps her friend was in some sort of trouble.

She looked up Natasha's number and dialled.

'Natasha?'

'Amanda, darling. I was going to call you. We didn't get any time to talk. Did you enjoy yourself? I had a wonderful time. And Adrian. Well he got off with this girl he swears she was double jointed.'

'It was fun,' Amanda said, wanting to change the subject. 'But I just wondered. Did you tell Maggie the details?'

'Tell Maggie? What do you mean? It was Maggie's friend.'

'Really?'

'Of course. She introduced us originally.'

'So she knew all about it?'

'Yes.'

'But she wasn't there, was she? I didn't see her.'

'Oh, she was there. But Jan gives her special treatment.'

'Jan?'

'The brunette with the permed hair.'

'What sort of special treatment?'

'A little bit of cheating. She gets to pick out whoever she wants before they go into the black room. Actually I think the black room is part of the thrill myself. All those groping hands . . . But how come you don't know all this. Didn't Greg tell you?'

'Why should Greg tell me?'

'My dear, I told you I was going to make a beeline for him. I got in the red group too. I was all set. Memorised everything he was wearing. We're all filing into the room when madam appears and yanks him away. Did you see her? Oh, no, you were still in the other room. Well, she did. I was furious, until I found this really talented girl. God, she was good. She had a tongue like a snake.'

'Maggie went off with Greg?'

'Exactly. Didn't he tell you? That's a bit naughty.'

Greg hadn't told her much about his evening. He'd mumbled something about a large woman with big tits and left it at that. He'd told her it wasn't much fun and he really didn't think there was any point going again. He seemed to have retreated right back into his shell.

'He's been busy,' Amanda said.

'I wish you'd bring him round. Or just come around yourself. We haven't seen Maggie for weeks, and now you. Why don't you come round this week some time? Any time, actually. Open invitation.'

'Great.' But Amanda couldn't muster much enthusiasm for the idea at the moment. She had other things on her mind.

She put the phone down and dialled Greg's. He had a private line and answered it himself.

'Hello.'

'It's me.'

'Hi.' He didn't sound very glad to hear her voice.

'I just wondered when you'd be home tonight.'

'Late.'

'How late?'

'Eleven, at least. There's this American in town. We've got to take him out to dinner. He's going to invest billions in the Canning Town development. Nothing I can do about it.'

'Why don't I come too? I could wear something short and show him some leg. Might get results.'

'No. No . . . ah . . . he's married. Happily married. It's a men only do. He'd be embarrassed if there was a woman there.' It was a weak excuse but he couldn't think of anything else on the spur of the moment.

'OK,' she said cheerily. 'See you later then.'

And that's when she knew the truth.

Amanda parked the hire car outside on a double yellow line at six o'clock. The company had an underground car park for their exclusive use and his car was parked in it. She could see the entrance ramp and knew there was no other way out.

As it happened she didn't have long to wait. At exactly six-fifteen his car nosed out of the ramp and waited until there was a break in the traffic. As he edged out into the road Amanda started the engine and followed him.

His office was in High Holborn. He drove into central London, the traffic at that time of the day making his progress extremely slow.

She didn't want to lose him so she stayed close to his rear bumper. She had worn a scarf over her head and dark glasses and with a strange car thought it unlikely he'd recognise her, even if he glimpsed her in his rearview mirror at a traffic light.

It was possible he was driving to the American's hotel. He would undoubtedly be staying at one of the five-star hotels on Park Lane and he was certainly heading in that direction. They would have cocktails, then dinner. Exactly as he had said.

He drove around the Mall and up to Piccadilly, which was consistent with visiting the Ritz, but then drove past and up to Park Lane which was consistent with any number of posh hotels. But then he swung around the back of the Dorchester and continued up Park Street to find his way into Manchester Square.

There was no trouble parking. Everyone had gone home by seven when he pulled the car into one of the parking spaces that surrounded the little garden of the Square.

It was easy for Amanda to park too. She locked her car quickly and ran after him on foot. There was a small hotel in George Street. It had a Georgian facade and a small, porticoed entrance.

The doorman saluted as Greg approached, appearing to know him.

Amanda hung back. He walked straight up the steps and into the hotel.

Some Americans were eccentric of course, preferring out of the way places, perhaps for sentimental reasons; somewhere they'd stayed the first time they'd come to London back in the good old days when they were young.

Leaving time for Greg to get inside Amanda walked over to

the doorman. 'That gentleman who just came in, the one with the navy suit,' she said. 'Do you know his name?' She slipped a five pound note into the palm of his hand.

The doorman looked puzzled.

'Mr Harvey,' he said.

'Thank you,' she whispered.

He had lied. He was using a false name and he had lied. She was sure he'd lied about other things too. He hadn't been working late last week. He'd been to this hotel.

She marched up to reception. 'What room is Mr Harvey in, please?'

'Oh, let me see.' The receptionist was young and pretty. She tapped the name into the computer. '210. Shall I call him for you?'

Amanda smiled her most endearing smile. 'I want to give him a surprise,' she said, putting her finger to her lips. That at least was true.

The girl giggled then went back to her work.

Amanda took a small lift to the second floor. A sign indicated that 210 was to the left. The corridor was short. She reached the door and listened. She could hear voices but could not hear what they were saying.

A chambermaid came around the corner with her cart, laden with all the things she needed to make up the rooms.

'Excuse me, miss, I've just done a stupid thing. Left my wedding ring in the bathroom and my husband's waiting for me downstairs. Could you save me having to go and get the key.'

'Certainly, madam. I'm always doing that myself. Take it off to wash and forget it. I'd forget my head if it weren't screwed on.'

She took her pass key and opened the door. Amanda smiled her thanks and went inside, closing the door after her.

She had expected a bedroom but found herself in the small hallway of what was obviously a suite.

The voices were coming from the door at the far end. It

was ajar. If she had any lingering doubts, if she imagined, for instance that the American had wanted his room hired in a false name for reasons of privacy and Greg had done it for him, they disappeared. She heard the unmistakable sound of sex. A woman's voice was crying out loudly with pleasure, each note louder and higher in pitch. She had heard precisely the same rising crescendo before.

Tiptoeing up to the door she eased it open silently and peered inside.

There on the floor by the bed was Maggie. She was on her knees, with her torso resting on the bed itself. She was wearing a bright red patent leather basque, patent leather stockings in the same colour and red patent leather high heels. Greg was kneeling behind her hammering his cock into her. From her position at the door Amanda could not tell which passage of her body he had availed himself of, but from the noise Maggie was making she was sure it was her anus.

Greg was fully dressed. She had evidently been waiting for him, dressed for sex. His need had been so urgent he'd barely had time to pull his trousers and pants down to his knees.

He plunged forward again. The force made her rear up from the bed and Amanda saw something hanging from her breasts. Two little gold clips were buried in her nipples, each attached to a thin gold chain. The final touch she thought, remembering the girl at the party. Perhaps she'd have her nipples pierced for him. She wriggled her bottom back against him, the chain quivering, then dropped forward on to the bed.

For a second Amanda thought of confronting them, then decided she had better things to do.

She let herself out of the suite, slamming the outer door as forcefully as she could to give them a start, then walked downstairs and used the telephone in the lobby.

The apartment block was only around the corner from Edington Street, one of those Victorian mansions made from red brick with large casement windows.

She parked the car, checked her hair in the rearview mirror, smoothed the sheer champagne-coloured hold up stockings she wore tightly against her legs to eliminate the smallest crease and wrapped her Burberry mac around her body. Not that it was raining. She stopped in Hyde Park to change, her gyrations in the back seat attracting the attention of three passersby and a dog.

There was an entryphone on the front door of the block which she didn't want to use so she waited until she saw someone coming out of the building and pushed in before the door could shut again. On the third floor she found Flat thirty-six.

She had considered all her options. She regretted losing Greg. She regretted it very much. But life had to go on. If her marriage was over there were at least other compensations. She could have phoned Annie and Phil. She could have gone around to Natasha and Adrian. Both would have found ways of taking her mind off her problems. But Alan had seemed the best idea. She had phoned Natasha and got Jan's number, then asked the woman for her brother's address.

There was a brass knocker on the door of the flat. She rapped it twice, loudly.

'Who is it?' a voice shouted after a moment.

'Delivery,' she shouted back.

She heard footsteps, heavy and fast. The door opened a crack then swung back fully. Alan stood to one side, his body dripping water on to the dark blue carpet, his loins covered with a miniscule towel.

His hand fell from the lock when he saw her. She pushed the door open then closed it behind her.

'You,' he said.

'I seem to have arrived at exactly the right time,' she said, eyeing his body.

'Is it raining?' he said looking at the mac.

'No but it's very wet,' she said. She pulled the mac off and let it drop to the floor. Apart from the champagne-coloured hold-ups she was naked underneath.

A Message from the Publisher

Headline Delta is a unique list of erotic fiction, covering many different styles and periods and appealing to a broad readership. As such, we would be most interested to hear from you.

Did you enjoy this book? Did it turn you on – or off? Did you like the story, the characters, the setting? What did you think of the cover presentation? How did this novel compare with others you have read? In short, what's your opinion? If you care to offer it, please write to:

> The Editor
> Headline Delta
> 338 Euston Road
> London NW1 3BH

Or maybe you think you could write a better erotic novel yourself. We are always looking for new authors. If you'd like to try your hand at writing a book for possible inclusion in the Delta list, here are our basic guidelines: we are looking for novels of approximately 75,000 words whose purpose is to inspire the sexual imagination of the reader. The erotic content should not describe illegal sexual activity (pedophilia, for example). The novel should contain sympathetic and interesting characters, pace, atmosphere and an intriguing storyline.

If you would like to have a go, please submit to the Editor a sample of at least 10,000 words, clearly typed in double-lined spacing on one side of the paper only, together with a short outline of the plot. Should you wish your material returned to you, please include a stamped addressed envelope. If we like it sufficiently, we will offer you a contract for publication.